Reflections of Feminism in Women Writers

Dr.M. Ananthi Devaraj

Published by

Reflections of Feminism in Women Writers

ISBN 978-93-86176-14-1

Author

Dr.M. Ananthi Devaraj

Bonfring
309, 2nd Floor, 5th Street Extension, Gandhipuram,
Coimbatore-641 012.
Tamilnadu, India.
E-mail: info@bonfring.org | Website: www.bonfring.org
Phone: 0422-4213231

Preface

The belief that women should be treated as potential intellectual equals and social equals to men. These people can be either male or female human beings, although the ideology is commonly associated with women. The basic idea of feminism revolves around the principle that just because human bodies are designed to perform certain procreative functions, biological elements need not dictate intellectual and social functions, capabilities and rights.

Feminism also by its nature, embraces the belief that all people are entitled to freedom and liberty within reason including equal civil rights and that discrimination should not be made based on gender, sexual orientation, skin colour, ethnicity, religion, culture or lifestyle.

<table>
<tr><th>S.No</th><th>Contents</th><th>Page No</th></tr>
</table>

S.No	Contents	Page No
1	Feminism	1
2	Indian Feminism	10
3	A Feminist Perspective of Virginia Woolf	40
4	Dalit Feminism	72
5	Black Feminism	79

FEMINISM

The word "Feminism" generally means "the belief that men and women should have equal rights and opportunities". It is also a planned activity in support of women's rights and interests. It is a collection of movements and ideologies aimed at defining, establishing and defending equal political, economic and social rights for women. The Endeavour includes in quest to establish equal opportunities for women in education or employments also. A feminist pleads or supports the rights and equality of women.

Feminism in India aims at defining, establishing and defending equal political and social rights as well as equal opportunities for Indian women. It is search for ensuing the women's right within the society of India. Like their feminist counterparts all over the world, feminists in India look for gender equality, such as the right to work for equal wages, the right to equal access to health and education, and equal political rights.

Indian feminists also have fought against socio-cultural issues within India's patriarchal society, such inheritance law and the practice of widow immolation known as 'Sati'.

The word Feminism first appeared in France and The Netherlands in 1872, Great Britain in the 1890s, and the United States in 1910. The Oxford English Dictionary lists 1984 for the first appearance of feminist and 1895 for feminism.

The term 'feminism' has its origin from the Latin word 'femina' meaning 'woman'. It refers to the advocacy of women's rights, status and power at par with men on the grounds of 'equality of sexes'. In other words, it relates to the belief that women should have the same social, economic and political rights as men. The term became popular from the early twentieth century struggles for securing women's suffrage or voting rights in the western countries, and the later well-organized socio-political movement for women's emancipation from patriarchal oppression.

The feminist ideologies began to influence the English literature in India. In the 20th century, women's writing was considered as a powerful medium of modernism and feminist statements. The majority of the novels depicts the psychological suffering of the frustrated housewife and oppressed lives of women of the lower classes. Feminism has been used by the women novelists. Their novels reflect that the present age women have realized that she is not helpless and is not dependent. They feel that woman is equal to man.

Nowadays, woman has become a money earner and she is not confined only to household works. Indian women writers explore the feminine subjectivity and apply the theme that ranges from childhood to womanhood. Through their novels, they told what actually feminism is. These women writers told that feminism means putting an end to all the sufferings of a woman in silence. Indian women writers have given a new dimension to the Indian literature. Indian English Literature has developed over a period of time and writing in English did not start in a day. It took many years to bring the present status.

We can find Indian literature as novels and also in the forms of poetries and short stories. Several women writers composed songs and short stories before the rise of novels. It is believed that women are the upholders of the Indian tradition of fables. In the middle of the 19th century, more women started to write in English language. During this period, more women actively participated in India's reformist movement against the British rule.

This led to the women's literature. At that time, their writings mainly concentrated on the country's freedom struggle.

Feminism is a social movement that purposes the equal rights and opportunities for women in society. It is a movement, which established by a group of women, whom we may call the 'feminists.' This group believes that western civilization is pervasively patriarchal that is male-centered and subordinates women to men in all cultural areas like family, religion, society, politics, economics and even art. Feminism is not only the movement, which run by women for women but it is a kind of Human liberation movement, which encourages society to think that women are also human beings.

Feminism is to look towards women as human beings and to think about their problems, dreams and needs. The debate between Western and Eastern feminism does not let you reach to the proper definition of feminism; rather it trapped us in an apple of harmony of wrong and right. We should change our views to look towards feminism by thinking over it in an isolated way, which is very necessary today.

Feminism in Indian literature, as can be most commonly conceived is a much sublime and over-the-top concept, which is most subtly handled under restricted circumstances. With advancement of time, however, feminism has been accepted in India, setting aside the patriarchal predomination to certain extent. Leaving aside the activists and crusaders of the political and social scenario, perhaps massive work of feminism is also consummate through Indian literature.

Yet, prior to comprehending a more extreme look into feminist literature in India, it is necessary to grasp the essential concept of the term `feminism` in the country's context, beginning from its inception.

Types of Feminism

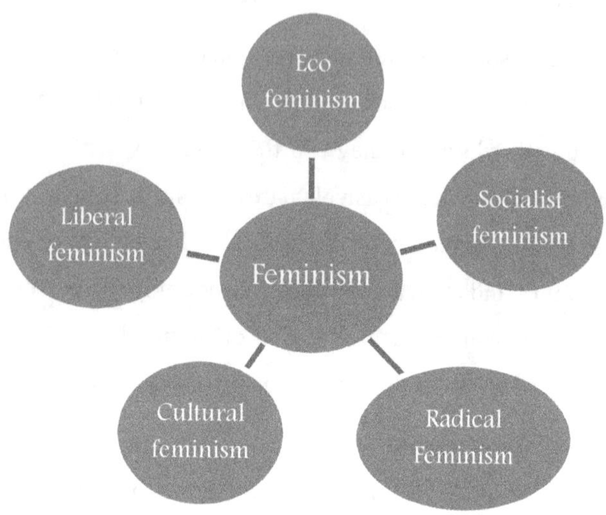

Liberal Feminism

It is the form of equality that disputes that equality for women can be achieved through legal means and social reform. It leans towards an equality or sameness argument with men. It conceives of politics in individualistic terms and looks to reform current practices in society. Liberal feminists are often seen among other types of feminists as traditional and tremendously white and middle class.

Cultural Feminism

Cultural feminism believes that a female nature or female spirit is important to society. There is fundamental personality and psychological differences between men and women and those women's differences are not only unique, but superior. This theory of feminism takes note of the biological differences between men and women-such as menstruation and childbirth.

Radical Feminism

Radical feminism is a branch of feminism that views women's oppression (which radical feminists refer to as "patriarchy") as a basic system of *power* upon which human relationships in society are arranged. It seeks to challenge this arrangement by rejecting standard gender roles and male oppression. Radical feminists locate the root cause of women's oppression in patriarchal gender relations, as opposed to legal systems (liberal feminism) or class conflict (like socialist or Marxist feminism).

Socialist Feminism

Socialist feminism focuses upon both the public and private spheres of a woman's life. Socialist feminism confronts the common root of sexism, racism and classism: the determination of a life of oppression or privilege based on accidents of birth or circumstances. Socialist feminism is an inclusive way of creating social change.

Eco Feminism

Ecofeminism is a social and political movement which unites environmentalism and feminism. Ecofeminists argue that a relationship exists between the oppression of women and the degradation of nature. Ecofeminists are concerned with connections between sexism and the domination of nature. They are also concerned with racism and other characteristics of social   inequality.

Black Feminism

Black Feminism basically argues that sexism and racism are inextricably linked. Black feminists argue that the liberation of Black women demand freedom for all people, since it would require the end of racism, sexism, and class oppression. Black women in this category often refer to themselves as womanize. Example-Alice Walker

Separatist Feminism

Separatist feminism is a form of feminism that does not support heterosexual relationships due to a belief that sexual inequality between men and women are irresolvable. Separatist feminists normally do not feel that men can make positive charity in the direction of the feminist movement and that even well-intentioned men emulate the dynamics of patriarchy.

Growth of Feminism

The basic of Feminism begin by Virginia Woolf in 1929. In her book "A Room of One's Own" Focus the need of liberation of women from the control of Patriarchal society.

First–wave feminism refers to a period of Feminist movement during the 19th and early twentieth century in the United Kingdom, Canada, the Netherlands and the United States.

Mary Wollstonecraft published one of the first feminist treatises, A Vindication of the Rights of Women (1792), in which she advocated the social and moral equality of the sexes. Wollstonecraft is considered as the grandmother of British Feminism and her ideas shaped the thinking of the suffragists, who campaigned for the women's vote. The majority of first wave feminists were more sensible and conventional.

The first wave of feminists, in contrast to the second wave, focused very little on the subjects of abortion, birth control, and overall reproductive rights of women. In the United States, it began during the early 1960s and lasted through the late 1990s. It was a worldwide movement that was strong in Europe and parts of Asia, such as Turkey and Israel it began in the 1980s, and it began at other times in other countries.

Whereas First wave Feminism focused mainly on suffrage and overturning legal obstacles to gender equality, second-wave feminism broadened the debate to a wide range of issues; sexuality, family, the work place, reproductive rights, de facto inequalities, and official legal inequalities. At a time when mainstream women were making job gains in the professions, the military, the media, and sports in large part because of second-wave feminist advocacy, second-wave feminism also focused on a battle against women's shelters, and changes in custody and divorce laws.

While, first wave of women's rights movement lasted from 1860 to 1920 with the attainment of franchise, variously called as Feminism or Women's Liberation Movement grew out of Civil Rights movement in America and student radicalism in Europe. Formal dating of new feminism coincides with founding of National Organization for Women (NOW) in 1966, under the famous author of The Feminine Mystique (1963), Betty Friedan.

Literature is human experience through imaginative writing, the early phase of feminism, was marked by autobiographical or even confessional writing which witnessed the relationship of literature to personal experience. It is through literature being a major cultural practice that feminism as critical theory as well as politics, developed after 1960. Many books appeared which, were works of literary analysts as well as of strong political arguments.

Second wave post 1920: Second wave of feminism saw a more major edge in feminist movement than was present in theories of earlier period. Radical feminists not only demanded equal rights but also declared superiority of women over men. They want women to be an intuitive, nutrient, supportive and sisterly whereas men are rational, competitive, aggressive and patronizing. They prioritized the battle against sexism to the battle against capitalism or that against legal and political reform that is liberal feminism.

In the starting years of the second wave of feminism or basic theoretical assumption was that the 'cause' of women's domination should be specified. Different feminists, however, offered different causes such as 'male control of women sexuality. But it was a common agreement that all women were oppressed or subordinated and reasons for their oppression lay in socially defined structures of patriarchy. This agreement however has given way to more varied set of ideas, which, arise from different sources.

In the 1980s and 1990s, feminist's social theory has sway the post-structuralism and post-modernist analysis. Following post-modernist emphasis on difference and plurality, feminist theorists have argued on difference and plurality Feminists theorists have argued that traditional feminist's analysis tended to reflect the viewpoints white women of North America and Western Europe. During post-Independent period feminism in Indian English literature was largely a of the western feminists movement.

Postmodernist and poststructuralist thoughts associated with feminist theories in a complex manner. While on the one hand feminism was fighting for equal subjects positions and had its roots in liberal humanist tradition, on the other hand it joined hands with poststructuralist theories of deconstruction as an oppressed and marginal viewpoint.

Third-wave Feminism Post 1950: Third-wave Feminism is a term identified with several varied strains of feminist activity and study. The movement arose as a response to the seeming failures and backlash against plan and movement created by second wave of feminism during the 1960s to 1980s, and realization that woman are of, many colours, ethnicities, nationalists, religions and cultural background. The third wave embraces sees diversity and change. In this wave, in previous ones, there is no all-encompassing single feminist idea.

Third wave feminism look for to challenge or avoid what it deems the second wave's essentialists definition of feminity, which often assumed a female identity and exaggerated the experiences of upper-middle class white woman. Third wave ideology focusses on more post-structuralism interpretation of gender and sexuality.Third wave theory usually incorporates elements of queer theory; anti-racism and woman-of-color consciousness; womanism; girl power; post-colonial; post-modernism; transnationalism; eco-feminism;individualist feminism; new feminist theory, transgender politics, and a rejection of the gender binary.

The Feminism of 19th and early 20th centuries focused on the acquisition of a few political rights and liberty for women. Such as right of the married woman to own the property and enter to contracts, the right. The Feminist thought and the feminist movements in the west had some influence on the woman's movement in developing countries like India.

Indian Feminism

To understand and sympathizes the sensibility of feminism it is important to observe that Indian feminist present altogether different picture sequence. The long and painful suffering of women, the bitter struggle for the exception of the idea of equal pay for equal work, the continuing battles on behalf of woman's right to abortion and to practice of birth control are some of the visible marks of the gender inequality that has persisted and that woman had to fight for inspire of the commitments they were made under circumstances.

Feminist situation in India possess a dissimilar dispensation. Indian society has always been highly hierarchical. the several hierarchy within the family concreting age, sex and ordinal position, congenial and fine relationship or within the community referring to the caste lineage, learning, occupation and relationship with ruling power have been maintained very strictly.

Describing the reaction to the feminist movement in India, Suma Chitnis writes, "The most distinctive features of this movement that it was initiated by man. It was only towards the end of the century the women joined the fray. The list of who, champion the cause of women is long–Raja Ram Manohar Roy, Ishwarchandra Vidya Sagar, Keshav Chandra Sen, Matahari, Phule, Agarkar, Ranade, Karve to mention a few. The record of the reform they undertook to achieve is impressive. It reveals that their efforts spanned action to abolish the practice of Sati, the custom of child marriage, custom of distinguishing widows, the ban on remarriage of the upper caste Hindu widows and many other civil practices that affected women. The feminist thought and feminist movement in the west have some influence on the woman's movement in the developing country like India. Yet, feminism as it exists today in India has gone beyond its western counter parts. Uma Narayan rightly puts it third world feminism is not mindless mimicking of western agenda in one clear and simple sense. Due to historical and cultural specifications of the region in India has to think in terms of its agenda and strategies.

In the Indian context several feminist have realized that the subject of women's invasion in India should not be reduced to contradiction between men and women. The woman in order to literate herself and advance needs to empower herself to confess different institutional structures and cultural practices that subject herself to patriarchal domination and comfort.

Indian writing in English is gaming ground rapidly. In the realm of fiction it has heralded a new era, has earned many laurels and abroad. Indian woman writers have started questioning the prominent old patriarchal.

Due to historical and cultural specifications of the region, the feminist movement in India had to think in terms of its Agenda and strategies. In the Indian context several feminist have realized that the subject of women's invasion in India should not be reduced to the contradictions between men & women. The woman in order to literate herself and advance needs to empower herself to confess different institutional structures and cultural practices that subject herself to patriarchal domination and comfort.

Traditionally, the work of Indian Women Writers has been undervalued due to patriarchal assumptions about the superior worth of male experience. The factors contributing to this prejudice is the fact that most of these women writers have observed no domestic space.

The Indian women's perceptions of their aspirations and expectations are within the framework of Indian social and moral commitments.

Indian Women Writers in English are victims of a second prejudice vis-a-vis their regional counterpart's. Proficiency in English is available only to writers of the intelligent, affluent and educated classes. Writer's works are often therefore, belong to high social strata and cut off from the reality of Indian life.

The majority of novels written by Indian women writers depict the psychological sufferings of the frustrated homemakers. This subject matter is often considered superficial compared to the depiction of the replaced and oppressed lives of women. Indian writing in English is now gaining ground rapidly. In the realm of fiction, it has heralded a new era and has earned many laurels both at home and abroad. Indian women writers have started questioning the prominent old patriarchal domination.

They are no longer puppets in the hands of man. They have shown their worth in the field of literature both qualitatively and quantitatively and are showing it even today without any hurdle. Today, the works of Kamla Markandaya, Nayantara Sahgal, Anita Desai, Geetha Hariharan, Shashi Deshpande, Kiran Desai and Manju Kapur and many more have left an indelible imprint on the readers of Indian fiction in English.

A major development in modern Indian fiction is the growth of a feminist or women centred approach, that seeks to project and interpret experience, from the point of a feminine consciousness and sensibility. Many Indian women novelists have explored female subjectivity in order to establish an identity. The theme is from childhood to womanhood-developed society respecting women in general.

Santha Rama Rau's' Remember for the House,' (1956), Ruth Prawar Jhabvala"s first novel 'To whom she will', 1955 and her later novel 'Heat and Dust' (1975)', Kamla Markandya's 'Two Virgins' (1994), Rama Mehta's

'Inside the Haveli' (1977), and Gaeta Hariharan 'The Thousand Faces of Night (1992)'.Are some of the leading women writers writing in Indian English literature?

The image of women in fiction has undergone a change during the last four decades. Women writers have moved away From traditional portrayals of enduring self- sacrificing women, towards conflcts, female characters searching for identity; no longer characterized and defined simply in terms of their victim status. A major preoccupation in recent Indian women's writing has been a delineation of inner life and subtle interpersonal relationships.

In a culture where individualism and protest have often remained alien ideas and marital bliss and the woman's role at home is a central focus. It is interesting to note the emergence of not just an essential .Indian sensibility but an expression of cultural displacement. Women's presentation is more assertive, more liberated in their view and more articulate in their expression than the woman of the past is.

Feminist Women Writers in India

The last three decade has seen the emergence of prominent Feminist in Indian Literature to begin with Shashi Deshpande.

Shashi Deshpandeis the second daughter of the famous Kannada dramatist in Karnataka and Sanskrit Scholar Shriranga. She did a graduation in Journalism at the Bharatiya Vidya Bhawan, Mumbai and worked for a couple of months as a journalist for the magazine 'On Looker'. Her first novel 'The Dark Holds No Terror' was published in June 1999. She is a winner of the Sahitya Akadami award, for her novel 'That long silence'. Her third famous novel is 'Roots and Shadows'. She has projected objectively a new female face with subjective experiences with a geocentric vision. She reflects on the problems and concerns of the middle class Indian women.

Her writings are rooted in the culture in which she lives. Her remarks are sensitive to the common everyday events and experiences and give an artistic expression to something that is simple and mundane. Her feminism is particularly Indian in the sense that it is borne out of the predicament of Indian women placed between contradictory identities. The women characters are with traditional approaches trying to tie family and profession to maintain the virtues of Indian culture.

Shashi Deshpande's novel 'A Matter of time' is a continuation of her exploration into the many facts of the feminine experience in writing. In this novel, she has displayed the themes of silence, gender differences, passive sufferings and familiar relationships into much deeper realms. It is a story encompassing three generations of women coming to terms with their life in and all female worlds.

The relation women characters share with their men is homered with silence, absence or indifference. The pain of disintegration of the family troubles Aru, who consider herself for her father's action and sets out to undo it. It is in this stifling atmosphere the characters evolve and come to a newer understanding of their lives. The role of fury and destiny are playing as main themes around which Deshpande weaves her tale.

Deshpande's simple yet powerful prose reads like a grandmother's tale that pierces the deep into heart and settles. At one point, the use of omniscient narration teases the reader as the speaker forces events but is not to share until time and plot unfolds it. Deshpande's 'A Matter of Time and Salman Rushdie's' Fury 'both novels spun around theme of existential fury. Deshpande brings Rushdie's novel out from howling New York City to a calm and mediating Karnataka and his hills in the gaps a reader might have had left craves for.

The underlying theme in Shashi Deshpande's novels is human relationships especially the ones that exist between father and daughter, husband and wife, between mother and daughter. In all relationships, the women occupy the central stage and significantly, the narration shifts through her feminine consciousness.

In her novels, three types of suffering women characters reoccur with subtle changes. The first type belongs to the protagonist's mother or the mother figure, the traditional woman, who believes that her place is with her husband and family.

The second type of woman is bolder more self-reliant and rebellious. She cannot confirm to mythological, submissive and surrender vision of womanhood. As radical feminist, ideology expressed, for example, Sarah's friend Nathan in the 'Dark Holds No Terror'.

The third, type of women characters, are the women in between neither traditional nor radical in their ideas and practice. For Example, Indu in 'Roots and Shadows', leaves her husband to seek refuge in her ancestral home. Being a woman herself, she sympathises with women. As Shashi Deshpande clarifies in one of the interviews about feminist approach in her writing,

The other, noted novelist under the study is Manju Kapur: a professor of English at Miranda House in Delhi. Her first Novel 'Difficult Daughters' received the Common Wealth Award for the Eurasian region. Her novel 'A married woman' is a seductive story of a love at a time of political and religious upheaval, and is told with sympathy and intelligence.' A Married woman' is the story of an artist whose canvas challenges the constraints of middle class existence.

Astha like to have a break from dependence on others and proceeds on the path of full human status that poses a threat to Hemant and his male superiority. However, she finds herself trapped between the pressures of the modern developing society and shackles of the ancient biases. She sets out on her quest for a more meaningful life in her lesbian relationship. She canonizes and commemorates her insulted feminine sensibility raising the male tantrum to social transformation in the society.

Manju Kapur in 'Difficult Daughters' presents the image of suffering women. In post-colonial era, partition has ever been the most prolific and prominent area for creative writers. During this phase, number of novels was written on the theme of the destruction. It brings the plight and provides a sad telling commentary on the breakdown on human values.

In her writings, Manju Kapur has emphasised on the issues in the context of patriarchy; inter-religious marriage; family bond, male-female bond, co-existence of past and present. She has narrated her women protagonists as a victim of biology, gender, domestic violence, and circumstances.

A major pre-occupation in recent Indian women's writings has been a delineation of Inner life and subtle relationships. In a culture where, individualism and protest have often remained alien ideas and marital bliss and the women's role at home is the central focus. It is interesting to see the emergence of not just an essential Indian sensibility but an expression of cultural diversion.

The other famous and renowned novelist under the study is Arundhati Roy, born in 1961 in Bengal. Arundhati grew up in Kerala; she trained herself as an architect at the Delhi school of Architecture but abandoned it in between. The International community knows Arundhati Roy as an artist with her debut novel The God of Small Things.'

'The God of small things' won Britain's premier Booker prize, the Booker McConnell in 1997. Roy is the first non-expatriate Indian author and the first Indian woman to have won this prize. Roy's major essays 'The End of Imagination' and 'The Greater common good' are available online. She is between the two Indian writers writing in English who has won the Booker Prize(the other one being Salman Rushdie for his 'Midnight Children'.)

Arundhati has never admitted that she is a feminist but 'The God of Small Things', reveals at many places her feminist stance and her protagonist represent feminine sensibility. Arundhati Roy's mother says, that Arundhati is a born talker and a born writer. While, she was studying in school, it was a problem to find a teacher, who could cope with her voracious appetite for reading and writing. Most of the time, she educated herself on her own.

Roy seems to be iconoclast in,' The God of Small Things'. The stylistic innovations make the novel unique and bring vitality and exuberance to the novel. The novel is unique in every aspect and it is a linguistic experiment with the English language. The stylistic writings include the use of words, phrases and even sentences from vernacular language, use of italics, subject less sentences, faulty spellings, topicalisation, deviation from normal word order, single word 'sentences,' change of word classes, clustering of word classes and a variety of other techniques. She has given prominence to ecology and subalternity as the major themes in the novel.

Roy's close observations and the minute aspects in the creation of her literary skills are observed in her other works. Her two important articles on the net are' The end of Imagination' and 'The Greater Common Good.' In the End of Imagination, Roy criticises nuclear policies of the Government of

India. Arundhati Roy foretells the harmful consequences of nuclear weapons on human beings and ecology in the End of Imagination.

Anita Desai, the other great novelist of the Indian English fiction was born in 1937.

Anita Desai is unquestionably one of the celebrated Indian-English fiction writers. She holds a unique place among the contemporary women novelists of India. She has to her credit a large number of creative works and a coherently growing readership throughout the world. She has published ten novels and other literary works of immense value.

Anita Desai's women characters in her novels rebel against patriarchal community in order to explore their own potential or to live on their own terms, regardless of the consequences that such a rebellion may have on their lives. They take the position of outsiders to fight and criticize those cultural ideologies that come in their way of becoming free individuals, self–chosen withdrawal, for these women, takes on the form a weapon for survival in a patriarchal community.

Desai's women, thus, want freedom within the community of men and women, as it is the only way that will succeed in fulfilling them In fact, Desai's model of an emancipated woman, Bimala in the novel Clear Light Of Day, is an unmarried woman. Her married women characters like Maya in Cry, a Peacock, Monisha in ,The City, Nanda in Fire in the Mountain, and Sita in Where Shall We Go This Summer? Become depressed, violent or self-destructive.

They either lose their sanity or kill others, or they kill or destroy themselves. The nemesis of these women is not a private one but an outgrowth of the complex social context, immediate family environments and the relationships with their men. Many of Desai's protagonists are portrayed as single women. Desai does not neglect the institution of marriage or support alienation from society.

Some of her women characters, like Tara in 'Clear Light of Day', do achieve fulfilment in their marriages Instead, through Bimala, Desai points to a kind of feminist emancipation that lies in not limiting women to their traditional roles but in expanding and awakening them to several other possibilities. Their kind of life, apart from being invigorating, also frees them from dependence on men. Bimala, through her individual freedom, exemplifies Simon De Beauvoir's description of an independent woman in her book.

Anita Desai's first novel, 'Cry, The Peacock' is concerned with its chief protagonist Maya's psychological problems. As a young sensitive woman, Maya wish to love and to live. She makes up the mind of her father, Gautama who is much older than she is. Maya is haunted constantly by the rationalistic approach of her husband to the affairs of life. Maya loves Gautama passionately and desires to be loved in return; but Gautama's coldness disappoints her.

This prophecy becomes troublesome to her unconscious mind. Anita Desai works on revealing the varying mental states, psychic observations, inner motives and existential pursuits of man. She succeeds fully in breaking non-grounds for her fictional art among her contemporary while dealing with the predicament of man and his social and moral dilemmas. Desai like Kafka unfolds the existential traits of man in society. She analyses a man in action in order to reveal his hidden motives behind the facial reality of conscious mind.

Now, let us discuss another popular women writer, Ashapurna Devi. She has focus on the revival of a reformed traditional womanhood that would accommodate women's need for self-expression. Like Desai and Bhandari, she considers education of women to be of utmost importance. She does so because she sees women, and not just men, as agents of female oppression.

Therefore, she is more critical of women than she is of men, who she feels are able to dominate women because dependent and insecure older women like mothers and mothers-in-law help them to do so. In her Trilogy, 'Pratham Pratishruti', Subarnalata and Bakul Katha. Ashapurna Devi traces the progression of the feminist movement from colonial to post-colonial periods in India.

She finds that the contemporary, educated and economically independent women, like Bakul in Bakul Katha, the last part of her trilogy, have become more self-centred than, the women of earlier generations, like Satyvati and Subarnalata in Pratham Pratishruti and Subarnalata respectively. More importantly and ironically, Ashapurna Devi finds that their freedom has not brought them closer to other women.

Ashapurna Devi advocates a re-vision of traditional community where the relations between men and women and between older and younger women are not based on the subservience of one to the other, but where women enjoy the same rights and privileges as men in an affirmation of human values. To get peace at home Ashapurna Devi wants women to break the walls of psychological imprisonment located inside them. The community, for Ashapurna Devi, should become the foundation that would free women by providing them the solid ground to stand firmly. She shows how the individual or smaller self finds liberation from pain and isolation.

Ismat Chugtai, the other prominent writer attracts our attention with her novel 'The Hearts Breaks Free', brings the story of oppressed people like Bua. Here, Chugtai shows the youthful, vital, nonchalant and exuberant Bua is in trouble, physically and in spirit, when she submits to the so-called reforming control of the traditional family. In contrast, rebellious Qudsia and Shabir, by isolating themselves from the traditional community, are able to find a new, fulfilling life.

Chugtai has vision of feminist utopia, which preserves the identity and happiness of the oppressed subjects.It is not conspicuously transformative as far as the patriarchal structure is concerned .What Shabir and Qudsia are able to achieve is a blissful separatist retreat from the world, an individualistic and subjective feminist utopia that does not offer any synthesis of sociality and individuality within the normative community.

Chugatai's novel openly reveals and reinforces the revolutionary and reconstructive features of their utopian community to the society. So that it can see how the outsiders' community function as a family in an extended sense, but it is different from the traditional Indian family where the men's and elders authority quickly takes over, and women are forced to earn merit by sacrifice. Some critics have raised concerns regarding the viability of such feminist utopias.

Chhaya Dattar and Popati Hiranandani try to create self-authenticating reflective spaces that liberate by disconnecting their women characters from their patriarch ally constructed social ties. Chhya Dattar, in her autobiographical story 'In Search of me', describes her experiences as a social worker in the tribal world. While recording, the unionized activities of the farm labours, who are mostly, women.

These women are cut off temporarily from her own feminist problems. Dattar experiences an inexplicable contentment that comes through the connection with one's self, symbolised in the story by the author's uninvited communion with tribal landscape that frees her, for those few days, from her social fears and uncertainties.

Dattar's response to her surroundings possesses a poetic and dramatic intensity that articulates her newly found energy and creativity and she begins to reconstitute her-self by looking at what has constituted her.

The act of analysing this discovery First part, strengthens her to exert her own agency over her controlling family members. Apart from the contemplative spaces, Dattar finds empowerment from watching the tribal women unveil their individuality, by using their voices to assert their concerns. Their individual invisibility begins to shatter as they try to make visible collective solidarity. The transformed spectacle, of the otherwise yielding tribal women into loud voices, clearly articulating their right to decent and respectful human hood, empowers the author to plan her own escape from the confinement of objectification.

Dattar, thus, shows that the individual spaces of feminist liberation are hinged on the interdependence of women. The collective solidarity of women, in Dattar's vision, punctuates the growth. It is unique and personal because power is derived from the collective vocal and active marginality.

Dattar's vision of feminist liberation provide avenues of becoming in the world as the registering of women's experiences, in her story, is framed by an engagement with their denial of dependence and self-sacrifice. Freedom, in the writings of both the authors, is primarily a mental phenomenon where women think to prepare for a transformation of consciousness.

Dattar provides images of feminist subjects, actively creating their own destinies and these images 'stand in contrast to the iconic figure of the female as passive, culturally fixed in an objective relationship in which she is always the inferior.

Bharti Mukherjee, the other post- colonial writer was born on July 27, 1940 at Calcutta she has done her M.A. in English and Ancient Indian culture from the Baroda University and her Doctor of Philosophy, in English and cognitive literature in 1969,From Lowa, university, United States.

Mukherjee's works focuses on the phenomenon of migration, the status of new immigrants and the feeling of alienation often experienced by expectation as well as an Indian women and their struggle. Her own struggle with identity first as an immigrant from India then an Indian expatriate in Canada and finally as an immigrant in the United States has led to her current contentment of being an immigrant in a country of immigrants.

Her important works are 'The Tiger's Daughter 1972' and 'Days and Nights'. The Tiger's Daughter is a story about a young girl named 'Tara' who ventures back to India after many years of being away to return to poverty and turmoil.

The second phase of her writing encompasses works such as 'Wife', 'An invisible woman' (Essay), 'The Sorrow and the Terror'. In 'Wife', (1975) Mukherjee writes about a woman named Simple who has been suppressed by such man and attempts to be the ideal Bengali wife.Out of fear and personal inability. She murders her husband and eventually commits suicide.

In her third phase, She wrote 'Leave it to me (1997)' Where she tells the story of a young woman named Debby Di Martino who seeks revenge on parents who abandoned her. The story reveals her ungrateful interaction with kind adoptive parents and a vengeful search for her real parents.

The novel also looks at the conflict between eastern and western worlds and at mother-daughter relationships through the political and emotional topics by the main character in her quote for the revenge.

Another renowned novelist of the modern Indian fiction is Kamala Markandaya born in 1924-she work under a pseudonym Purnaiya Taylor. She was a graduate of Madras University. She moved to Britain after India's Independence and is known for writing about cultural clashes between Indian urban and rural societies. Markandya has published her first novel, 'Nectar in a Sieve' (1955)'. It is a bestseller and considered a notable book by the American library Association.

Her other works are 'Some Inner Fun (1965)', A Silence of Desire (1961), Possession (1963), A handful of Rice (1966), The nowhere man (1972), The Rising (1973), The Golden Honey Comb (1977) and Pleasure City (1982).

Kamala's 'Nectar in a Sieve' is about a strong hero, character by the name of Rukmani. As she narrates her story, the readers are involved in her pain. Losing sons and seeing herdaughter became a prostitute, Rukmani still stands strong. Rukmani the main character and her daughter Ira display suffering through the novel. Rukmani works hard and is devoted to her gentle husband. Rukmani has faced Poverty, famine, and divorce of her barren daughter, the deaths of her sons, her daughter's prostitution and finally her husband's death.

Kiran Desai born in 1971 is an Indian author who is citizen of India and a permanent resident of the USA. Her novel 'The Inheritance of loss' won the 2006 Booker prize and the National Book Critics Circle fiction award. Her first novel 'Hullabaloo' published in 1998, won 'Betty Trask Award', a prize given by the society of Authors for the new novels by citizens of the Common Wealth of nations under the age of 35.

'The Inheritance of Loss' opens with a teenage Indian girl, an orphan called Sai, living with her Cambridge educated Anglophile grandfather, a retired judge, in the town of Kalimpong on the Indian side of the Himalayas.

Sai is romantically involved with her maths tutor, Gyan, the Descendant of a Nepali Ghurkha mercenary, but he eventually recalls from her obvious privilege and falls in with a group of Ethnic Nepalese insurgents.

Kiran Desai has handled several major issues of modern civilisation in her second novel. The concept of globalisation is multisided. It has economic, political, social, cultural and educational aspects. It may create an opportunity or a danger, because of Globalisation, situations have changed, new concepts have emerged and people have stepped out their areas of confinement to find company and competency among their counter parts.

Nayantara Sahgal was born in 1927 and is an Indian writer in English. Her fiction deals with India's elite responding to the crises engendered by political change. She was the first female Indo-Asian writer to receive wide recognition.

Her main works are:

1.   Prison and chocolate cake (memoir), 1954
2.   This time of morning, 1965
3.   Storm in Chandigarh, 1969
4.   The day in shadow, 1971
5.   Rich like us, 1988
6.   Lesser breeds, 2003

It shows that women writers have gone up from difficult to tribal and rural areas too, but all of them have expressed their concern for women and their problems. The variety of subjects, they have touched upon is a great contribution in creating awareness for the modern women all over the globe. The variety of subjects handled by them considering Indian environment needs an appreciation. Some of the writers have not claimed that they belong to feminist's movement yet their writings suggest that their inner spirit and feelings are for the welfare of the women only.

Shobha De, a supermodel, celebrity journalist and the well-known author stands as a pioneer in the field of popular fiction and ranks among the first to explore the world of the urban woman in India. With her extraordinary ability, she presents very sensitive aspect of human life. Her way of narrating every aspect of human relationships is wonderful. Really, she is frank in narrating the incidents and situations with a touch of open heartedness.

The most famous Indian woman novelists along with De are Kamala Markandaya, Anita Desai, Bharti Mukherjee, and Shashi Deshpande. Among these women writers, De is entirely different. She has given importance to women's issues and they are dealt with psychology in her style of intimate understanding. Her novels indicate the arrival of a new Indian woman, eager to defy rebelliously against the well-entrenched moral orthodoxy of the patriarchal social system.

Eager to find their identity, in their own way. Her female characters break all shackles of customs and traditions that tie them in the predicaments and rein in their freedoms and rights. They are not against the entire social system and values but are not ready to accept them as they are. Her female characters are modern, strong and take bold decisions to survive in society. This secures her position in literature as a feminist novelist.

Money symbolizes power and freedom and a room of her own is to have contemplative thinking. Very often women had enjoyed these things in the past so to develop their imaginative capabilities and personal freedom.

Women were not recognized as individuals or autonomous beings. Women had to face many obstacles in the academic circuit, which symbolize the effects of an educational culture that radically restricts the scope of women's intellectual exposure. Woolf identifies the certain information of being denied access to buildings or ideas as another type of infringement on the freedom of the female mind.

It is observed that men have written many books about women but no book has been found on men either by male or female authors. The male authors highlight the strength and weakness of women. They did actually celebrate the virtues and vices of women. They had been written in the red light of emotion and not in the white light of truth. Ashraf Behan first entered into the world of art and earned through writing. She was forced to earn her livelihood when she lost her husband. Women abstained from the world of imagination so to look after their household duties.

Women work a lot from early morning to late night; still their work is not being paid. Women have served all these centuries as looking glasses possessing the magic and delicious power of reflecting the figure of man at twice its natural size. Art did not give way to activism in the writings of men, as they were more or less didactic. In contrast, women were more concerned with activism as a tool of social change.

Activism is an "effective agent of social change than electoral politics". Women writers believed that art is a major weapon for social change .Many of the women writers have moved towards the noble profession of activism through art. The word activism is synonymous with protest or dissent and more deliberately, it is an international action to bring social change. Activism in literary writers is a new phenomenon, where they dedicate themselves to the welfare of the society.

Many of the literary writers advocate activism as a part of their writing, since they believe that writing has a social purpose. It is only through art and activism that a radical change can take place for the good of the society. Women writers like Mahasweta Devi, Sara Joseph and Arundhati Roy consider as a major source of inspiration to pave its way to activism. They are all socially committed to serve the humanity and extend their helping hand to the poorest of the poor.

Mahasweta Devi, the renowned Bengali writer and activist, was born in 1926 at Dhaka in East Bengal, the modern day Bangladesh. She had done her elementary studies at Dhaka and after the partition of Bengal; her family migrated to West Bengal in India. She took the B.A (Hons) in English from Vishvabharati University in Shantiniketan. She passed the M.A in English as a private student from Calcutta University in 1963.

Mahasweta Devi started writing from a very early age and contributed various articles to newspapers and magazines she belongs to a family that has an ardent love for literature and social work. Her father Manish Ghatak was a poet and a novelist and her mother Gayatri Devi was a social worker and a writer.

Mahasweta Devi was inspired by her family to pursue her career as an artist and an activist. She was appointed as a lecturer in English at Calcutta University and was retired from service in 1984. After the retirement, she concentrated on writing for the upliftment of the poor, especially the downtrodden sections of the society. She has been editing the quarterly 'Bortika'since 1980 to voice the pent-up emotions of the marginalized people of India.

Mahasweta Devi established herself as the major novelist during the second phase of her creative writing. In Kavi Bandyoghita Gayiner Jivan O Mritya, Mahasweta Devi portrayed the inner struggles of a lower caste boy to fight against human rights. Mahasweta Devi deals with radical left Naxalite movement and its effects on the people.

There was a major shift in the third phase of Mahasweta Devi's creative writing, art gave way to activism and she tried to depict the struggles of the people against exploitation and tyranny. Arranger Adhikar was based on the life and struggles of Birsa Munda, who could give a befitting fight to the British forces in the famous Munda rebellion of Nineteenth Century. Mahasweta Devi got the Sahitya Akadami award in 1979 for this work from the Government of the West Bengal.

The subject of her creative writing has remained struggle of socially marginalized, the poor and the tribes. The tribal, who contribute 8 per cent, and the so-called scheduled castes, which belong to the bottom of India's caste hierarchy, along with other depressed communities, meet these criteria as no other social category in this country does. They remain the focal point of her writing.

Mahasweta Devi has created an indelible mark on her fictional and non-fictional writings. In her fictional works, Mahasweta Devi has included a wide range of topics, such as demands for law, minimum wages, roads, schools, drinking water and various oppressions against the minorities. Mahasweta Devi insisted on the need for literary campaign in tribal areas and she carried out this mission with the help of educated people in the locality.

She has played a crucial role in forming various organizations among the tribal as the first step for development. These organizations have been functioning as a source of inspiration to tribal and they are able to raise their aspiration in public. She could put an end to 'bonded labour' system that was prevalent at Palamau District in Bihar with collective force of the organisation.

Sara Joseph is the forerunner of feminist movement in Kerala. She is an artist and activist of the present generation. She was born in 1946 at Kuriachira in Thrissur. She was married at the tender age of 15 when she was in class IX. However, she was allowed to attend her classes even after marriage. Sara Joseph initiated her artistic career by writing poems, which she did as a ninth standard student.

One of her poems was published in the Mathrubhumi weekly. She could write poems even after her marriage and all together 15 poems were published. Sara Joseph was very often invited to recite her poems in the formal get together of the poets. The renowned Malayalam poet Vyloppilly advised her to concentrate only on poems and avoid fiction. Sara Joseph's literary career rests on all kinds of genres with a major thrust on short stories and novels.

She could pass the S.S.L.C examination in the first class and later she was sent to the Teacher's Training Course. She began to earn money, as she becomes a teacher. She was driven by an ardent force to complete her studies and she did her B.A and M.A in the first class as a private candidate. The public Service Commission appointed her as Malayalam Lecturer in Government Sanskrit College, Pattambi, where she got the opportunity to face realities of life. She then realized the need for changes a society through education.

Sara Joseph established herself as a leading novelist in Malayalam language through her trilogy: Alahayude Penmakkal being the first, the second being Maatathi and the third is Othapp. Sara Joseph began her artistic career very early in her life. She brought out her first collection stories Manassile Thee Maathram in 1973 and collection of stories in Kaadinate Sangeetham in 1975.

Sara Joseph won the Kerala Sahitya academy Award in 2001 for her first novel Alahayude Penmakkal and she received the Kendra Sahitya Academy Award in 2003 and Vayalar Literary Award in 2004 for the same novel. Sara Joseph's second novel Maatathi bagged the first O Chand Hu Menon Award, Abu Dhabi Arang Award and Kuwait Kala Award in 2004.

Sara Joseph devotes most of her time for the upliftment of the marginalized sections of the society. She has proved that art and activism could go hand in hand to bring changes for the eradication of poverty, rejections of patriarchal ideologies and male dominated culture, campaign against deforestation and the creation of the eco - friendly environment .As a mark of protests, Sara Joseph avoids all kinds of inorganic things in her life. She advocates woman's autonomy through education and self–employment.

Sara Joseph initiated her artistic career by writing poems, which she did as a ninth standard student. One of her poems was published in the Mathrubhumi weekly. She could write poems even after her marriage and all together 15 poems were published. Sara Joseph was very often invited to recite her poems in the formal get together of the poets. The renowned Malayalam poet Vyloppilly advised her to concentrate only on poems and avoid fiction .Sara Joseph's literary career rests on all kinds of genres and the major thrust is given to short stories and novels.

In Alahayude Penmakkal Sara Joseph immortalized the fast disappearing local dialect of Thrissur. She tells the story of a group of people who are deprived of their native land because of urbanization. Her creative writing is a protest against Globalization and exploitative culture. The small world presented in her novel Alahayude Penmakkal has now become a global phenomenon where the marginalized sections of the community gives the way to others.

Sara Joseph upholds the philosophy that art and activism are the essential means of social change. The role of an artist is to keep the people informed of the various developments that take place in the society and prepare them to form their perspective about it. Sara Joseph was being severely criticized by others for blending art and activism in her writing.

In the opinion of critics, activism affects the aesthetics of literary work, and they themselves suggests that Sara Joseph's earlier works are better than the later one's. It is remarked that her earlier works are deprived of primitive tone and that the later ones reflect the social realities of life in general.

The advent of 'Gynocriticism' resulted in the need for creating a new language for women .The feminists believe that the existing language is created by the male chauvinistic world. As a result, it is difficult for women to represent some of the male gender terms. In Malayalam, there is an equivalent male gender term for 'Vaishya', which means a prostitute.

The existing structure of the language needs to the dismantled to undermine the power within the male gender. The difference one observes in women writings, the first step towards the liquidation of patriarchal ideologies. In her novel' Othapp,' the central character Margareta tries to reject even the male dominated religion by way of performing priestly duties.

The concept of the 'other' is as primordial as consciousness itself. In the most primitive communities, one finds the expression of a duality, that of the 'self' and the 'other. The patriarchal culture considers women as an 'object '. The word 'Charak' for instances, is used in Malayalam to refer to a woman as a commodity to be used sexually. Such derogatory terms have been used by the society for the objectification of woman.

Sara Joseph strongly disapproves the so-called Fashion Shows by woman. It is part of Patriarchal culture, where women become more sex objects in front of others. On the other extreme, the male dominated society would always encourage woman to keep up her femininity. Simone de Beauvoir had done a lot of research on women and her thesis was found in the Celebration of femininity by the practical culture is actually a subjugation of female autonomy.

In order to destroy the supremacy of patriarchal culture, human beings should be identified as male and female based on their sex and not as men and women. The term 'woman' connotes the quality of woman, which the society attributes to a female. She should be obedient, patient and servile in her behavior towards others. The moment a woman does something different than the society would call her either a bad woman or lunatic. Human beings are not products, which come out of a factory to be alike. It is high time that the patriarchal culture ceased to exist for the all-round development of women.

Chitra Banerjee Divakaruni, an Indian-American award winning author and poet who migrated to America in 1976 at the age of 19, witnessed the troubles faced by the so-called black in a country of the so-called white. As an expatriate, she is conscious about her own identity and hence her works reflect the sense of rootlessness and alienation, which are mostly relevant to the Indian diaspora.

Disparity in a new land persuaded her to establish *Maitri*, a hotline for South Asian women who were the sufferers of discrimination, cruelty and abuses. The initiative taken to improve the condition of such women motivated her to write *Arranged Marriage*, a work of art to narrate the tale of abuses and bravery of immigrant women. Chitra Banerjee Divalaruni possesses a high rank in the contemporary circle of Indian Diaspora for being a very keen observer of life of the Indians, especially Bengali women, in the United States of America. Through the characters of her stories in *Arranged Marriage*,

Divakaruni explores the problems of identity crisis, emotional isolation and non-communication, the experience of migration, etc. Her books have been translated into 29 languages, and her works have appeared in over a hundred magazines and anthologies. Several of her novels and stories have been made into films and plays. Before she began her career in fiction writing, Divakaruni had established herself as an acclaimed poet and wrote poems encompassing a wide variety of themes.

Her main area of focus is once again immigrant experience as (Divakaruni Profile by Arthur J. Pais) Chitra Banerjee Divakaruni, the author of several award-winning volumes of poetry and novels, in her debut collection of short stories, *Arranged Marriage* (1995) which has also won a PEN Josephine Miles Award and a Bay Area Book Reviewers Award, deals with the immigrant experiences, especially of women in general.

Divakaruni, with her remarkable workmanships portrays diasporic women protagonists, living in two cultures, struggling the insecurities of exile, and questioning their identities. In this brilliant collection, which contains eleven short stories, Divakaruni's focus is mainly on women caught between two worlds, their dejection, and disillusionment and adaption to such conditions.

Besides, it evaluates their attitude and approach toward life, abandonment or preservation of their cultural values. Each tale has a freshness and uniqueness of diasporic consciousness. In the majority of the stories, the author skillfully narrates the stories of Indian women immigrants living in the perpetual socio-psychological conflict.

Chitra Banerjee Divakaruni belongs to the first generation of Indian immigrants in the United States who has spent a part of her life in India and has carried the baggage of her native land offshore. She has keenly observed the postcolonial society of India as well the challenges of diaspora abroad. With this observation, she has portrayed the fear of adjustment, struggles and sufferings of her characters, both from India and abroad, authentically.

The focal point in almost all stories in *Arranged Marriage* is the problem of adjustment arising from cultural variation experienced by an Indian woman when she moves toward the west, which is in important theme in the mosaic of American Indian culture. The first story of the collection, "Bats" talks about the physical and emotional sufferings and the courage of an Indian woman who leaves her torturer husband and returns home with her child in India.

The second story of the collection, "Clothes", which is about the unfulfilled promise of a marriage, also talks of unknown fear of migration and adjustment of Sumita, the central character, who has to accompany her husband to California. When she moves from Calcutta (now Kolkata) to California just a week after her marriage, she understands more about the place and its culture mostly from her husband, Somesh, who works with his partner in a store called 7-Eleven, selling all kinds of amazing things- apple juice, American bread, potato chips, beer, and wine:

People migrate to foreign lands with the expectations of liberty, gratification, and existence which clashes with the traditional values of their homelands. Caught in between two different worlds, they struggle to maintain their cultural values and adapt themselves in the new environment. Sumita, an Indian bride, living in America, has constantly been fed on traditional ideas that it is her moral duty to act like a good Indian wife...serving tea to her in-laws friends..covering her head with her sari...not addressing her husband by his name, etc.

The traditions Sushmita follows are all signs of respect in India and are strictly maintained in her home in California. Such situations make her impatient and remind her of her homeland, India. Sumita"s life in America is not different from the life led by other daughter-in-laws in Indian society yet, she doesn"t want to go back to India, her motherland, even when her husband is murdered at his shop as now it would be much difficult for her to adapt herself to her roots than to live in a dangerous land.

Similarly, Jayanti in "Silver pavements, Golden Roofs faces the dilemma of being an immigrant when she migrates from Calcutta to Chicago to live with her aunt Pratima and uncle Bikram. Jayanti, being the first generation Indian-American, cherishes her past and its memories as an indispensable, integral part of her root and being. The apartment, in which she has to live with her aunt and uncle, is no better than to the house Jayanti came from.

Like other diasporic writers, Divakarini writes about,, human predicament" and the crisis of identity in the alienated land of America though she has made it her homeland. Identity crisis, alienation, and nostalgia are the chief characteristics of her writings. It is the painful anguish of diasporic identity and the sense of alienation that Divakaruni focuses on in her collection of short stories, *Arranged Marriage.*

In the story "Silver Pavements, Golden Roofs" Jayanti who came to America with bright dreams, expresses her bitter experience of being immigrant, recalls an incidence when a group of boys shouted at her and her

Pratima aunt with racist slurs and attacked them with the „fistful of slush". Jayanti, who was proud to be an upper class Indian, questions her relation to American race categorization and her entire perception of her own race is thrown into question after this incidence.

Though this incidence made her to long for her home in Calcutta desperately, she can't stop thinking of„ the pink-tipped blond hand of the air-hostess" who offered her a warm towelette and all American hands that she knew will keep coming back in her dreams. The sense of belonging to a particular place and culture and at the same time being an outsider to it creates an inner tension in the characters of Chitra Banerjee Divakaruni.

An immigrant like Jayanti is compelled to live between two worlds: the imaginary and the real, the past and the present, and the virtual and the material. While standing on the balcony of her aunt"s apartment in a snowy weather, Jayanti realises that the „excruciating pain" of chilly snow falling on her hands fades away when she dreams of her life in America and makes sense.

The clash between cultures and the conflict between family and career, which affects immigrant women largely, are interwoven with the other diasporic consciousness in *Arranged Marriage.* Women in diasporic situations struggle with the material and spiritual insecurities of exile on the one hand, and the demands of family and work with the claims of old and new patriarchies on the other. They experience the spatial, cultural, and emotional vacuum in their efforts to settle and adapt themselves in a new land.

In "Perfect life", Meera, an Indian girl, rejects the traditional roles of a wife and a mother in favour of her career and education in America. However, after meeting a six-year old orphan boy, Krishna, she begins to contemplate motherhood and even to adopt the child and raise him by herself. She envisages the child"s first day of school, trip to Disneyland and baseball games, and could see herself as the actual mother of the orphan. Now she understands motherly love quite well.

Caught up in her new role as a mother, Meera after the disappearance of Krishna from the Foster Homes office, considered quitting her job and started distancing herself from her boyfriend, Richard, and even thought to inform her mother in India to consider her an arranged marriage with a widower. But she never posted the letter. Even though she was crazy with anger, sorrow and guilt, she knew that would have been a bigger mistake than the ones she"d made already.

Loneliness and disillusionment are the burning problems of the expatriate community in the nation of their choice. In the story "Affair", Abha recalls how Meena, her close friend, failed to adjust because she found herself lonely and isolated in the over-involvement of professional commitments of her husband, Srikant. Abha used to reveal her friend"s loneliness.

Further, Abha recalls the secrets of Meena"s loneliness: "...how she still turned on the TV evenings when Srikant was late coming back so she wouldn"t have to listen to the silence, how she slept with the light on when he went out of town" (240). Meena"s loneliness intensifies after her first miscarriage. This loneliness brings her closer to Ashok,

Under the sway of emotions, now Meena had no fear to share her most intimate joys and fears even with Ashok, Abha's husband. Keeping aside the consequences and ignoring Abha"s isolation and anguish unconsciously, Meena enjoys the company of Ashok just to overcome the frustration of her isolated life. Abha, on the other hand, suffers from uncompromising insecurity.

In "Meeting Mrinal", the last story of *Arranged Marriage*, Asha is envious to see her childhood friend, Mrinal enjoying freedom of movement, power, and economic security in England but soon is disillusioned of her perfect life when Mrinal admits. The disillusionment about perfect life of Mrinal and the pang of loneliness and dejection in her own life made Asha cry who has been divorced by her husband, Mahesh and who is not getting along too well with her teenage son, Dinesh.

The women of these short stories experience a conflict of consciousness and struggle to define themselves like those of several South Asians and Americans. In the private realm, the traditional Indian culture women have to perform some specific duties and follow strict norms of morality and are transgressed only by those considered daring and depraved.

A Feminist Perspective of Virginia Woolf

Virginia Woolf was born in 1882, the youngest daughter of the large and talented Stephen family. Her father, Leslie Stephen, was a distinguished critic, biographer, and philosopher. He was one of the most influential figures in the literary world of late Victorian England. Her mother, Julia Stephen, was a daughter of the novelist William Makepeace Thackery.

She born Leslie Stephen's four children: Vanessa, Thoby, Virginia and Adrain. Virginia Woolf was destined to be a writer. Though Woolf was denied the formal education allowed to males, she was able to take advantage of her father's abundant library. She used to meet great writers such as Thomas Hardy and William Thackery.

The tranquillity of Woolf's family life was shattered by series of mental breakdowns attributable to many sad events. The first one was the death of her mother in 1895. Two years later, Stella Duckworth, her stepsister, died. After the death of her mother and step-sister, Woolf was subjected to her father's endless demands for sympathy and attention from his daughters.

At the same year of her half-sister's death, she began her first diary. Over the next seven years, her decision to write began. Woolf suffered another mental breakdown combined with scarlet fever and attempted to commit suicide. When she recovered, she and her siblings moved to Bloomsbury.

Virginia Woolf was a member of a group known as Bloomsbury Group that included her brother, Thoby, and a brilliant young group of Cambridge graduates. It included Lytton Starchy, Maynard Keynes, Clive Bell, E.M. Forester, and Roger Fry. This circle constantly expanded to include new friends such as T.S. Eliot, Katherine Mansfield, Elizabeth Bowen, Vita Sackville-West and her husband Sir Harold Nicholson.

In this intellectual stimulating environment, Virginia Woolf pursued her literary interests, but her life was interrupted again by the sudden death of her brother, Thoby, who died of typhoid on a trip to Greece in 1905. Virginia Woolf got married to Leonard Woolf. He recognized his wife's extraordinary talents from the beginning, and provided her with the encouragement and protection she needed to fulfill her literary promise. Leonard founded the Hograth Press in 1917, which was developed to be one of the most successful and innovative publishing houses of its time.

Virginia Woolf suffered from gloom, depression and madness. Her work was interrupted by periods of physical and mental illness. She couldn't tolerate the absurdity of life. She was under the influence of the psychological stress caused by war. She feared that her madness would return and she would not be able to continue writing. Woolf committed suicide by drowning herself in a river in March 1941.

Virginia Woolf's novels show an intellectual commitment to political, social and feminist principles. Woolf was one of the writers whose view of life was conditioned by the forces of their age. She had acute awareness of the damage of the contemporary life, and her writings condemned the British patriarchal culture. In her novels, Woolf intended to portray a satiric picture and terrible indictment of the English social system.

She found that the emotional strain of modern life almost damaged the bonds of communication among people. She asserted that personal relationships provide the order and meaning in life, but with the traditional values of life, loss of meaning and social relevance, human relationships have suffered a serious blow.

This state of confusion is expressed in Woolf's novels through her characters' inability to communicate with each other.

In *Mrs. Dalloway, (1925),* Clarissa tries to discover a means of communication with others, but she fails to overcome her sense of loneliness. In *To the Light House (1927),* though the Ramsays and their guests live together, each is an isolated soul. Woolf dedicated her novels to analyze the miseries and loneliness of women's lives that have been shaped by the moral, ideological and conventional means.

Miss Kilman and Rezia are outstanding examples of the cruelty of the blind social political doctrine of the English society. She aimed at creating an androgynous world in which there is a balance between intellect and emotion. Woolf introduced women characters who signify hope in this world such as Elizabeth in *Mrs. Dalloway* and Lily in *To The Lighthouse.*

Feminism can be roughly defined as a movement that seeks to enhance the quality of women's lives by defying the norms of society based on male dominance and subsequent female which implies the emancipation of women from the shackles, restrictions, norms and customs of society. It demands that women should be treated as autonomous subjects, and not as passive objects. It seeks to achieve equality between men and women in moral, social, economic and political fields.

The objective of that movement is the creation of a new identity for women and making them aware of their rights. Before the mid of the 19th century, women were considered weak intellectually and physically. Such concept was consolidated by social conventions. According to that concept, society was divided into two worlds: private and public world.

The private world implied that women should stay at home. They were not allowed to work or learn. They were educated only in a way that suited their claimed weak nature such as sewing, nursing and painting. The sole vocation for women was marriage. According to that role, women couldn't revolt because of fear, shame and rejection by society. The public world implied that men are strong mentally and physically. They were allowed to work, and were given proper education such as mathematics and science, etc.

The sole vocation of men was to work and build society. That formula of dividing the world into two worlds was against human nature. Accordingly, it led to the emergence of several feminist groups which attempted to provide solutions to women's question. The feminist groups could be classified into liberal, Marxist, radical, psychoanalytic, social, existentialist and post-modernist. None of them has developed a comprehensive answer to the feminist question.

But such coordination and understanding among them can make feminists achieve their goals, and help them eradicate women's sufferings concretely. According to the liberal feminists, the cause of women's oppression lies deep in traditions and false moral codes. They demand that women should be provided with proper education and economic equality with men.

Mary Wollstonecraft called for re-organizing society and educating women in order to develop them morally and intellectually. J.S. Mill, argued that women are in need of the same civil liberties and economic opportunities as men, and that men should work for liberating women and changing the traditional way of their thinking. Marxist feminists stressed that capitalism is the primary source of women's oppression.

They demanded that the capitalist system must be replaced by a social one, in which means of production belong to all. The existentialist feminist Simone De Beauvoir, in her book, The *Second Sex (1940)*, demanded that women should choose whether they become mothers or not. She called women to create a special world for themselves, and demanded that women should read books by great writers like Virginia Woolf and Catherine Mansfield.

In her opinion, women should be independent financially and autonomous professionally. For radical feminists, the oppression of women is rooted in the patriarchal system. They demanded that society must be purged from legal, social, political and cultural principles of patriarchy. Psycho-analytic feminists found the source of women's oppression is hidden deep in women's psyche. They called women to probe the depth of their psyche in order to evaluate their position as women.

Post-modern feminist argued that the more feminist thought they have, the better. Helen Cixous argued that women write differently from men because of their biological differences. She believed that, by developing a feminine writing, women would change the way the world thinks of them and their place as well. Julia Kristeva differs from Cixous. She rejected Cixous' identification of the masculine with biological men and the feminine with biological women. She thought that boys can be identified with their mothers, and girls can be identified with their fathers.

Girls can write in a masculine mode, and boys can write in a feminine mode. Social feminists thought that psychology, patriarchy and capitalism determine women's destiny, so the oppression of women is rooted in social, economic, and psychological factors. It implies the need for self organization and change in gender identity. They developed two approaches to provide a comprehensive answer to the women's question: dual and unified.

The dual approach feminists believed in that was any change in the status of women should be accompanied by the defeat of capitalism and patriarchy. This can be achieved by changing patriarchy's economic aspects through material means and its social and ideological aspects by nonmaterial means, psycho –analytic means. The unified approach took both defeat of capitalism and patriarchy in one direction.

The unified approach feminists argued for that is if women were equated with men, regarding the same division of labour and the same fee, they would be equated with men regarding the same value and status. They argued that the division of labour analysis has the conceptual power to change Marxist –feminist theory which is powerful enough to accommodate the ideas of Marxist, radical and psycho-analytic feminists in a unitary framework.

Social feminists unveiled the reasons and suggested a comprehensive answer for women's oppression. At Woolf's time, people were affected by the collapse of the old concepts and values that influenced the entire conceptual world. Virginia Woolf had acute awareness of the ravage and demolition of the contemporary life. The human nature underwent a change in her writing after the shock of the First World War. She criticized the authoritarian power that made autocrats of husbands and fathers.

Virginia Woolf was subjected to a depressive atmosphere and patriarchal rule in her family. She was affected by her father's domination of his wife and daughters. In Marcus "New Feminist Essays on Virginia Woolf Ellen Hawks comments on woolf's view towards her mother. It was the woman, the human being whose sex made it her sacred duty to sacrifice herself to the father, whom Charlotte Bronte and Elizabeth Barrett had to kill.

After the death of her mother and half-sister, her father's demands and needs for sympathy and attention from his daughters increased. She was also affected by the sexual expression of power and manipulation of her step-brothers. Her strong admiration for women was coupled with growing dislike for males' domination, represented by her father and step-brothers especially by George and Gerald.

She and Vanessa formed a league together and united against the depressing atmosphere and patriarchal rule in their family. On the basis of this relationship, Woolf appreciated the need for women's friendship and continued to insist on the importance of women's friendship against patriarchal machinery.

Being aware of the importance of the need for all women to rebel against the patriarchal system, Woolf examined the literary works and biographies of women writers such as Elizabeth Barrett Browning, Jane Austen, Charlotte Bronte, Mary Wollstonecraft, Russell Mitford and others. She examined their lives and the way they translated their resentment of males' dominance in literature.

She discovered that killing the stereotyped feminine, the angel of the house, as Woolf called her, was a part of the occupation of women writers. These women writers maintained their integrity, and insisted upon their own identities against patriarchal society. She believed that the artist needs shared goals, tradition and continuity.

Virginia Woolf found that women were excluded by men from being the makers of these masterpieces, so she created for women a female tradition in "A Room of One's Own" *(1929).* In order to kill the angel and create an artist, women should create their own identity, talk about their own experiences and encourage women's writing. Some of Woolf's friends were central to her development of politics such as Margaret Davies, president of the National Women's Co-operative Guild, and Janet Case. Woolf recognized that women might change society's values and save it from self-destruction.

Virginia Woolf called for recognition of what she had seen in her friendship with women-the characteristics that would have protected them from emotional exploitation. She called for a world of sympathy. She called for a society of women as an alternative to authoritarian structures. In her call, she bids women to believe in themselves, maintain integrity of their values and exclude from society all masculine values of hierarchy, dominance and power.

In her short story *A Society (1920)*, she talked about a group of women who join together to investigate the masculine world. Hawkes comments onWoolf's view in the story, Woolf stresses the most important lesson to be learned by women, not from men but from each. As the narrator, of the story tells one of the members of the society.

Woolf worked for and was influenced by several feminist groups such as the Suffrage Movement, World Women Organization, National Union of Women's Suffrage Societies and Women Cooperative Guild. Social feminists believed in the distinctiveness of women's values and capabilities. Virginia Woolf's views can be considered identical to those of social feminists. She argued that women who give life are not so careless of it and women's socialization would keep a government run by women from being imperialistic.

Virginia Woolf was, actively, an interested writer of the feminist question. In her writings, she calls women to express themselves in all professions open to humanity.

Virginia Woolf dedicated her major novels to analyze the patriarchal English society.. She portrayed different types of women in various contexts. She opened women's eyes on their inferior status and provided them with a female tradition to rely on. She strived to provide women with the proper clues for having a meaning in life. She believed that such meaning would lead to a purpose in life, and thus it would create a modern and normal life.

In *A Room of One's Own*, Woolf tries to answer the question of why there have been so few female writers. She refers this to women's minor status largely to socio-economic factors; especially their poverty and lack of privacy. Woolf also exposes gender-consciousness. She believed that it cripples both male and female writers. She posits that men historically belittle women as a means of asserting their own superiority.

Men are threatened by the thought of losing their power, so they disparage women to glorify themselves. Consequently, women's writing is marked by the feelings of anger and fear, and men's writing is marked by aggression. In her feminist essay *Three Guineas (1938)*, Woolf sets them a part from the patriarchal world and recommends that women must be in league together against patriarchy for the creation of a healthy and normal life.

Mrs. Dalloway

Woolf portrays the impact of the patriarchal society of England on women's lives. She portrays the loneliness and frustration of women's lives that have been shaped by the moral, ideological and conventional factors. The action of Mrs. Dalloway is confined to a single day in June. On this day, Clarissa gives a party in the evening. Peter Walsh comes unexpectedly and calls upon her.

The party brings together several other friends from her young days: Sally Seton, Whitbread and others. Clarissa is a middle-aged woman, over fifty and the wife of Richard Dalloway, a conservative member in the parliament. They live in West-minister, a rich and fashionable locality of

London. Clarissa holds the centre of the stage, and her experiences of love are part of every warp and woof of the novel.

There is her love-story with Peter Walsh, Richard Dalloway and Sally Seton. The most important love-story of Clarissa's life was that with Peter. Whenever she thinks of the past, of Bourton, the town where Clarissa lived with her parents before marriage, she thinks of Peter. She loved Peter when she was a young girl and still loves him. Memories of Peter keep coming to her mind throughout the novel. After she had refused Peter's offer of marriage, he went to India, and married another woman, but that marriage didn't turn out to be a happy one. At the age of fifty-two, he fell in love with a married woman.

The relationship between Clarissa and Peter starts with love, but it has been marked with a sense of tension. Clarissa's soul craves for love and to be loved, but also wants privacy and independence of her own. In her relationship with Peter, her soul underwent a constant tension between love and individual freedom. Clarissa wants to preserve her virginity. She equates virginity with freedom as a result of an aggressive social structure where women were snubbed and despised.

Peter is portrayed as a male dictator who believes that he has the right to dictate to her how she should live and what she should do. Clarissa thought that if she had married Peter, he would have engulfed her and forced her soul. She gives reasons for rejecting him and marrying Richard. For in marriage a little licence, a little independence there must be between people living together day in day out in the same house; which Richard gave her, and she him. But with Peter everything had to be shared, everything gone into.

(Mrs. Dalloway, P.10) Clarissa feared intimacy with Peter, and was unwilling to share him her feelings and thoughts. She was attracted and frightened at the same time. The reason behind not marrying Peter was her apprehension that he would not give her the kind of freedom that she thought essential for her happiness. On the other hand, Peter thought that she was cold and lacked female sympathy. He couldn't understand the importance of her emotional need.

Peter is unconventional and visionary in society. He can't fit into the conventional society of London. He is able to see the worldliness, hypocrisy and insecurity of his society. In his youth, he aspired to be a brilliant poet. He was deeply interested in the affairs of the world. It was the state of the world that interested him; Wagner, Pope's poetry, people's characters eternally, and the defects of her own soul.

On the other hand, Clarissa possessed nothing except giving parties. Not that she thought herself clever, or much out of the ordinary... She knew nothing; no language, no history; she scarcely read a book now... Her only gift was knowing people almost by instinct, she thought, walking on. (Mrs. Dalloway, P. 11).

Clarissa is not a visionary in society like Peter. She gives parties and likes to bring people together. She regards her parties as an offering, though she doesn't know precisely to whom. She compensates her need of warmth by giving parties and seeking the warmth that other people offer. Clarissa vacilates between her need of love and her need of independence. She lacks depth of feelings and understanding, and can't see the inward troubled soul of society. She only sees the world's glittering body, but she knows nothing about social problems. This tendency in Clarissa seems to Peter to be excessive, and has made him say that she would prove to be the perfect hostess. He thinks that she cared for rank and society. He sees through Clarissa the hypocrisy and insecurity of the society of London. He always scolded her and said sarcastically that she would marry a Prime Minister and stand at the top of a staircase.

Clarissa felt such comments were pretty hurtful and often wept. The perfect hostess he called her (she had cried over it in her bedroom), she had the makings of the perfect hostess, he said. (Mrs. Dalloway, P. 10) Consequently, their relationship ended in failure. In "Mrs. Dalloway", Clarissa's relationship with her husband hasn't proved to be successful.

Throughout Virginia Woolf's presentation of Clarissa-Richard marital relationship, she emphasizes that marriage is not a guarantee of a happy relationship and mutual understanding between a husband and a wife in patriarchal society, even while living under the same roof.

Clarissa rejected Peter because his love was too possessive and domineering while Richard's is not. In her decision to marry Richard, she chose privacy over passion. But whenever she thinks of Richard, she automatically thinks of Peter. Clarissa tries to feel convinced that she acted wisely in rejecting Peter, but the virtues she attributes to Richard as a husband are obviously representing a pathetic attempt to view her married life as a total success.

So she would still find herself arguing...still making out that she had been right-and she had too- not to marry him... ...she was convinced; though she had borne about her for years like an arrow sticking in her heart the grief, the anguish. (Mrs.Dalloway, P. 10) Clarissa lacks effusiveness and generosity. She can't respond to male demands of sympathy and is unable to provide her husband with the kind of romantic passion usually expected in heterosexual relationships.

She chooses an attic room as a refuge from the traditional female role. This kind of marital relationship caused a state of loneliness and lack of intimacy in marriage. Loneliness without any sense of partnership with the husband is suggested through the narrow bed. Clarissa has to mitigate her loneliness through social life and idle gossip. She has come to accept that there is a gulf even between husband and wife.

The following conversation presents an evidence of the casual nature of Clarissa-Richard relationship: Some committee?' She asked, as he opened the door. 'Armenians,' he said; or perhaps it was 'Albanians.

(Mrs. Dalloway, P. 132)]] This conversation shows also that Richard is so preoccupied with politics more than his wife. In response to his loyalty to the social duties of upper class, he leaves his wife for a meeting that he does not care about.

Again we find Richard invited to Lady Bruton's party without his wife. This action fills Clarissa with a sense of emptiness Richard is excluded from Clarissa's room and insists on her resting undisturbed because of a heart affliction. Clarissa mocks her husband's attempt at taking a hot water bottle as a substitute for her warmth: And if she raised her head she could just hear the click of the handle released as gently as possible by Richard, who slipped upstairs in his socks and then, as often as not, dropped his hot-water bottle and swore! How she laughed! (Mrs. Dalloway, P. 37)

Naik cited in Aston (1998:114) explains Woolf's view on this incident between Clarissa and Richard: Woolf interprets Richard's withdrawal from his wife, Clarissa, as an attempt to impose strictures, on female desire under the garb of medical impositions by disinterested men of authority in medical profession.

Virginia Woolf called for excluding all masculine values of hierarchy, competition and dominance. She called for the society of women as alternative to the authoritarian structures, and insisted on the importance of women's friendship against these structures. Woolf found a refreshing freedom and mutual understanding in her relationship with women. She found it so secret and private compared with men.

Virginia and Vita Sack- West experienced astonishing revelations with each other and Woolf wrote about it truthfully in Mrs. Dalloway: It was a sudden revelation, a tinge like a blush which one tried to check and then, as it spread, one yielded to its expansion, and rushed to the farthest verge and there quivered and felt the world come closer, swollen with some astonishing significance, some pressure of rapture, which spilt its thin skin and gushed and poured with an extraordinary alleviation over the cracks and sores.

Then, for that moment, she had seen an illumination; a match burning in a crocus; an inner meaning almost expressed. In her youth, Clarissa, sought for the society of women. She couldn't resist sometimes yielding to the charm of a woman, not a girl, of a woman confessing, as to her they often did, some scrape, some folly. And whether it was pity, or their beauty, or that she was older, or some accident- like a faint scent, or a violin next door (so strange is the power of sounds at certain moments), she did undoubtedly then feel what men felt. Only for a moment; but it was enough. (Mrs. Dalloway, P. 36)

Clarissa's love for Sally Seton was the most intense emotion she will ever experience. Woolf expresses this kind of relationship in the following words: The strange thing on looking back, was the purity, the integrity, of her feeling for Sally. It was not like one's feeling for a man. It was completely disinterested, and besides, it had a quality which could only exist between women, between women just grownup. It was protective, on her side, sprang from a sense of being in league together. (Mrs. Dalloway, PP. 38-9)

Sally was anti-patriarchal woman. She asserted herself as a woman and demanded equal rights for women Sally was Clarissa's inspiration to think beyond the walls of Bourton, read and philosophize.

Woolf describes Clarissa-Sally relationship as a gift: She felt that she had been given a present, wrapped up, and told just to keep it, not to look at it- a diamond, something infinitely precious, wrapped up, which, as they walked (up and down, up and down), she uncovered, or the radiance burnt through, the revelation, the religious feeling! (Mrs. Dalloway, P. 40)

Clarissa broke the authorial patriarchal voice as uniting with women results in equal relationship. This kind of relationships was a reaction against patriarchy and for the creation of a society for women.

Though Clarissa was attracted to Sally, she was stifled by the traditions of society. Sally Seton represented the forbidden in patriarchal society, and her vision was not shared and accepted by the narrow-minded people of the world. People like Sally aren't welcomed by society, and they are compelled to conform and resign. Her acceptance of the social roles and constraints of respectability prevented her from following her union with Sally.

Her defeat and acceptance of these roles are clear in her reaction to the thought of a woman becoming pregnant before marriage. Sally mentioned that the housemaid had married the neighbouring squire and had given birth before marriage. Peter considers Clarissa's reaction as the death of her will. He could see Clarissa now, turning bright pink; somehow contracting; and saying,' Oh, I shall never be able to speak to her again!' Whereupon the whole party sitting round the tea- table seemed to wobble. It was very uncomfortable........'The death of her soul.' He had said that instinctively, ticketing the moment as he used to do-the death of her soul. (Mrs. Dalloway, P. 66)

Sally Seton was also compelled to yield and accept the patriarchal forces. She got married to a rich industrialist and resigned to be a conventional mother. Both Clarissa and Sally were defeated because the only accepted female identity was the one that was accepted by patriarchy.

We are introduced to Miss Kilman who has a grudge against the world. She lost her job as a school-teacher when the war came because she was suspected of having German sympathies. She felt that she had been cheated, and wanted to have revenge against the whole world. The cruelty of life drove her to seek solace in the church. Religion for her is a choice of despair. She failed to get that solace because the church didn't help her in mastering the raging passion of hatred.

While religion teaches love, it could not fulfill its purpose of anchorage. She felt that she would have triumphed on this grim reality only by humiliating Clarissa. In humiliating Clarissa, she wants to humiliate the cruel world that knows nothing about her suffering and poverty. Under the pretext of religion,she is obsessed with the thought of possessing Elizabeth's soul. Miss Kilman hates Clarissa because she views her as a product of the patriarchal society by which she was victimized.

Miss Kilman's grudge against Clarissa is expressed effectively in the following words: If she could have felled her it would have eased her. But it was not the body, it was the soul and its mockery that she wished to subdue; make feel her mastery. If only she could make her weep, could ruin her; humiliate her; bring her to knees crying. (Mrs. Dalloway, P. 138)

This thought makes her repress her femininity by dressing like men, behaving with ruthlessness and adopting aggressive masculine values. An example of the unconventional woman is portrayed through the character of Elizabeth Dalloway. Elizabeth has ambitions to have a career and a professional life. She has planned to be a doctor, farmer, or to go into Parliament.

The disintegration and lack of mutual understanding which mark her parents' relationship have their impact on her own life. Her father fails to recognize her at the party. When he does, he accepts her as a decorative object- a part of the trivial feminine world. Her mother feels shocked, and helpless on finding her daughter under Miss Kilman's influence all the time.

Clarissa's helplessness as a mother is expressed, with a sudden impulse, with a violent anguish, for this woman was taking her daughter from her, Clarissa leant over the banisters and cried out, 'Remember the party! Remember our party tonight.' But Elizabeth had already opened the front door; there was a van passing; she didn't answer. (Mrs. Dalloway, P. 139)

Elizabeth has to choose between participating in the trivial feminine society of her mother or taking part in the male dominated society. None of these choices is adequate example for the creation of a modern woman. But blending the emotional side of Clarissa with the ambitions of the professional life of Miss Kilman gives a promise for the birth of a new identity for women.

Lady Burton is an aristocratic woman and a representative of patriarchy. She is proud of her ancient decent, social status and style of living. She has an ambition to solve social and political problems. Lady

Bradshaw is a classical example of the upper class Victorian woman. She obeys her husband and responds fully to his effort to attain power and domination over her. She keeps herself busy in the trivial life of attending dinner-parties.

In *Mrs. Dalloway*, the dark picture of patriarchal society is portrayed through Septimus-Rezia relationship. Septimus had gone to war with a sense of total dedication to the ideal of freedom which was seriously threatened by the German hordes. The grim experience of war has given him a new vision of the truth. He is able to see the painful reality of English society and wouldn't accept the world as different from what he actually sees it.

This vision of Septimus makes him an insane person through his doctors and people's eyes. He married Rezia without loving her because he couldn't stay alone at night. Rezia suffers silently and alone. Her husband rejects to have a child because he rejects to join patriarchy by becoming a father himself.

Rezia finds herself alone in a foreign country without a husband or a child. She was very lonely, she was very unhappy! She cried for the first time since they were married. Far away he heard her sobbing; he heard it accurately, he noticed it distinctively; he compared it to a piston thumping. But he felt nothing. His wife was crying, and he felt nothing; only each time she sobbed in this profound, this silent, this hopeless way, he descended another step into the pit. (Mrs. Dalloway, P. 100)

Woolf compares Rezia to a flower attempting to protect her battered husband with her maternal petals: Sitting close, sitting beside him, he thought, as if all her petals were about her. She was a flowering tree; and through her branches looked out the face of a lawgiver, who had reached a sanctuary where she feared no one; not Holmes; not Bradshaw; a miracle, a triumph, the last and greatest. (Mrs. Dalloway, P. 163)

Rezia tries to restore her marriage. She refuses anyone to separate her from her husband, but Dr. Holmes, the agent of death pushed his way up to Septimus, who jumps to death, and Rezia is driven to darkness and destruction. Septimus's death is a moment of vision for Clarissa. She comes to understand that Septimus, in his madness, has denied society and its constructing conventions that have imprisoned her into a snobbish hostess. Woolf depicts Clarissa's final apprehension of the truth of life:

A thing there was that mattered; a thing, wreathed about with chatter, defaced, obscured in her own life, let drop every day in corruption, lies, chatter. This he had preserved. Deathwas defiance. Death was an attempt to communicate, people feeling the impossibility of reaching the centre which, mystically, evaded them; closeness drew a part; rapture faded; one was alone. There was an embrace in death. (Mrs. Dalloway, P. 202)

Clarissa feels a shamed of her past and ignorance of the painful nature of life. Somehow it was her disaster-her disgrace. It was her punishment to see sink and disappear here a man, there a woman, in this profound darkness, and she forced to stand here in her evening dress. She had schemed; she had pilfered. She was never wholly admirable. Odd, incredible; she had never been so happy. Nothing could be slow enough; nothing lasts too long. (Mrs. Dalloway, P. 203)

To the Lighthouse (1927) is concerned with the Victorian arrangement of patriarchal society, and it questions the distinction between men and women's social roles. Throughout the novel, we find that there are two distinctive worlds: the world of men, the masculine, and the world of women, the feminine. The masculine is marked by egotism, rigidity, and insistence on intellect over feeling. By contrast, the feminine is marked by imagination, intuition and compromise. The patriarchal society has discouraged mixing the characteristics of these two worlds, and thus prevented the creation of a modern society, in which there is balance between the masculine intellect and the feminine emotion. Mrs. Ramsay represents the conventional and the submissive female to patriarchal society.

Her medium is emotion and her form is human relationships. Lily Briscoe is a representative of the unconventional and rebellious against gender boundaries. Her medium is intellect and her form is her painting. Through Woolf's projection of Mrs. Ramsay's life and her relationships to men characters, she affirms the female values of fertility, giving and creating harmony, which is associated with Mrs. Ramsay; but Woolf criticizes the way she has chosen to subject her positive femininity to masculine definitions.

Woolf's projection of Lily's life and her relationships to Mrs. Ramsay and male characters is an attempt to teach women to accept their femininity, cultivate their masculinity, and choose the role that they want to play as independent women. Examining the lives of these two female characters, we find Woolf seeking to integrate the masculine and feminine qualities into a balanced whole that would render men and women the capacity to achieve meaning in life. Ramsays' marriage is a patriarchal marriage based on middle–class Victorian values .

We find inadequacy in this marriage which doesn't allow mature intellectual interchange. The character of Mr. Ramsay is based on Woolf's father, Leslie Stephen. Marcus comments, according to Leslie, It was a natural law that a wife should have no legal rights, no right of her own property or money, no training for any job, nor any hope for obtaining one.

Mrs. Ramsay is subordinated to his needs and engulfed by his world. She has been badly crippled by her narrow education and trained to be intellectually inferior. Charles Tansley says that women cannot write and paint Marcus (1981: 152) comments that being trained to be intellectually inferior has the desired effect on Mr. Ramsay.

The stupider the wife appears to the husband, the more desirable she becomes. Yet Mrs. Ramsay is not as stupid as her husband thinks of her. She is frightened of her potential of intellectual achievement, but she never had time to read books. His wife's stupidity makes him see her astonishingly beautiful.

Yet Woolf expresses her view regarding this matter through Lily's consciousness, Beauty was not everything. Beauty had this penalty–it came too readily, came too completely. It stilled life –froze it. One forgot the little agitations; the flesh, the pallor, some sight or shadow, which made the face unrecognizable ... It was simpler to smooth that all out under the cover of beauty. (To the Lighthouse, P.193)

Hypocrisy is evident in Mr. and Mrs. Ramsay's interaction. Mrs. Ramsay subdues herself to her husband because she suspects her husband's intellectual abilities. Mr. Ramsay wants to reach the heights of genius, the letter Z, and to be like Shakespeare. He has no questions about the division of social roles which have shaped the relationship between husband and wife in a patriarchal society.

Accordingly, his lack of the feminine qualities of creativity denies him an access to the forces of life. He wants to be assured that he lives in the heart of life. His need of sympathy renders him reliant on his wife's femininity. He comes to her not only for sympathy but to feel that he is needed over the world. Mrs. Ramsay looking at the same time be animated and alive as if all her energies were being fused into force, burning and illuminating, and into this delicious fecundity, this foundation and spray of life, the fatal sterility of the male plunged itself, like a beak of brass, barren and bare. He wanted sympathy. He was a failure, he said. (To the Lighthouse, PP. 42-3)

Mrs. Ramsay doubts her husbands' intelligence, but she doesn't let herself, even for a second, to feel finer than him. She doesn't discuss her husbands' intellectual problems, but she takes the role of fulfiller to his needs and makes him dependent on her femininity. But it was their relationship, and his coming to her like that, openly, so that anyone could see, that discomposed her, for the people said he depended on her. (To the Lighthouse, P.45)

Such hypocrisy between husband and wife raises an accusing finger at patriarchy which imprisons the intellectual maturity of their husbands. Mr. and Mrs. Ramsay are aware of the irremovable barrier which separates them. They had nothing to say, but something seemed, nevertheless, to go from him to her. It was the life, it was the power of it. It was the tremendous humour, she knew, that made him slap his thighs. Don't interrupt me, he seemed to be saying, don't say anything; just sit there. And he went on reading. (To the Lighthouse, P.129)

Woolf emphasizes the separation between Mr. and Mrs. Ramsay: He turned and saw her.' Ah! She was lovely, lovelier now then than ever.' He thought. But he couldn't speak to her...He passed without a word, though it hurt him that she should look so distant, and he couldn't reach her...again he would have passed her without a word had she not. (To the Lighthouse, P.172).

Both Mr. and Mrs. Ramsay accept the limits of their marriage .In their silence, they want certain barriers to be maintained. Mrs. Ramsay has a mania for arranging marriages. She insists that Minta must marry and she wishes to create something that lasts between Paul and Minta. She succeeds in getting them in marriage, but their marriage fails. Paul had come in and gone to bed early. Minta was late.

There was Minta, wreathed, tinted, garish on the stairs about three o'clock in the morning. Paul came out in his pyjamas carrying a poker in case of burglars... He spoke indignant, jealous words abusing her...she flamboyant, careless. For things had worked loose after the first year or so; the marriage had turned out rather badly. (To the Lighthouse, PP.187-8)

Mrs. Ramsay thinks of another marriage between Mr. Bankes and Lily. Yet Mrs. Ramsay doesn't succeed in getting them married. She thinks that Lily is unwomanly. Mrs. Ramsay can't understand that being womanly means no longer being defined by one's relation to men or one's reproductive system. Mrs. Ramsay pities Mr. Bankes for being unmarried. Mrs. Ramsay succeeds in bringing Mr. Bankes to her dinner party, but she fails to fulfil his need for intimacy and unity.

Mr. Bankes is not satisfied with the emotional aspects of Mr. Ramsay's life. He feels they have weakened Mr. Ramsay's potential .For Mr. Bankes, family life is at odds with intellectual life. He finds that Mr.Ramsay's life vacillates between his sterile thought and fertile wife. In Mrs. Ramsay's party, her superficiality bore Mr. Bankes. This makes him not attracted to the domestic life of Mrs. Ramsay; since it is not satisfactory to his need of fulfilment. Mrs. Ramsay herself is stuck by the same questioning of Mr. Bankes in the party.

At this moment, all affection for her husband is momentarily gone, and all what she wants to believe and create is gone. She comes to question her status as a woman. But what I have done with my life?...The room was very shabby...nothing seemed to have emerged. They all sat separate. (To the Lighthouse, PP.90-1) Mrs. Ramsay has sometimes the skill of making men feel good. That is because she makes them feel superior. She feels satisfied when they feel proud through her admiration of them.

Ironically, men need women's acknowledgment of their worth, and only through their admiration they can feel proud. At the dinner party, Tansley doesn't enjoy Mrs. Ramsay's effort and sees through her superficiality. His insecurity, regarding his feelings of his social inadequacy, prevents him from understanding how to socialize effectively. Mrs. Ramsay pities him and forces Lily to stop bothering him.

The novel stresses the antagonism between the father, and his children. James, the youngest of Ramsays' children looks forward to making a trip to the Lighthouse. Mrs. Ramsay promises him to go tomorrow if the weather were fine. Yet James's hope is dashed to the ground by his father's saying that the weather will not be fine. Then, Woolf describes James's rage against his father: Had there an axe handy, a poker or any weapon that would have gashed a hole in his father's breast and killed him, there and then, James would have seized it. (To the Lighthouse, P.8)

Mrs. Ramsay feels angry about her husband's abnormal concern for his children's feelings and she tries to comfort James compassionately. She is infuriated by her saying and calls it the folly of her mind. The reason for his anger is that he thinks that Mrs. Ramsay gives a false hope which was utterly out of the question. But in this way, Mr. Ramsay turns into a symbol of tyranny and despotism in his children's eyes. Mrs. Ramsay tries to make her children more tolerant and more sympathetic. She regrets that her children will grow up in this atmosphere. She doesn't want them to grow up in a terrible and hostile life.

Lily Briscoe is a representative of unconventionality. Her rebellion against the given social roles is demonstrated in her pursuance of truth. Yet, under the expectations of the feminine role in patriarchal society, Lily undergoes self–division. She is divided between her inspiration for the world of self-actualization and the limitations of the maternal world.

Consequently, Lily's divided self imprisons her femininity and places restraints on her relationship with men. She finds feminine roles unfulfilling. She is afraid of her femininity and denies it. Lily feels guilty and insincere about being forced to relieve Tansley in the party. Lily fights these limitations through her art, but she can't achieve fulfilment. She is confused in regard to a romantic relationship with Mr. Bankes. She understands its beauty; but on the other hand, she fears its degradation. In the dinner party, she says to herself, She needn't marry, thank Heaven, she needn't undergo that degradation. She was saved from that dilution. (To the Lighthouse, P.111).

Lily Briscoe likes and admires Mr. Bankes. She feels a shamed of her impulse towards him and, at the same time, wants to compliment him, but she doesn't say anything. Unlike Mr. Bankes, Mr. Ramsay lacks the ability to understand and admire the feminine.

Lily criticizes this in Mr. Ramsay in comparison with Mr. Bankes. After the death of Mrs. Ramsay, Mr. Ramsay demands Lily's sympathy. Yet he expresses his need as a desire to give her.

Instead of giving sympathy, Lily compliments his boots. Lily associates giving with femininity and she refuses and revolts against men's need of sympathy. Yet Mr. Ramsay respects the compliment and smiles. Now Lily has made advance to Mr. Ramsay as an equal, not a woman to man, but as a man to man. He can see her now as a person interested in similar things.

Mr. Ramsay acknowledges that she admires his traits rather than she fulfils his need for sympathy .At this moment, Lily's role is about being an ungendered equal and Mr. Ramsay's need for sympathy diminishes. Lily's confusion drives her to assert her gender through her painting, and to find the truth inside herself. Yet, Lily is unable to define her femininity and yearns to the security of the ideal woman, Mrs. Ramsay. She wants to express Mrs. Ramsay's idealization of her painting, but Lily knows that Mrs. Ramsay's idealization is an illusion.

Her inability to accept her femininity and Mrs. Ramsay's idealization prevents her from establishing a vision of truth in art. Ten years after Mrs. Ramsay's death, she recalls Mrs. Ramsay's life and comes to cherish in herself powers different from those that motivated Mrs. Ramsay for imposing harmony and order in life. The memory of Mr. Ramsay is a catalyst for Lily's growth. She realizes that her thoughts about Mrs. Ramsay's life have imprisoned her and crippled her talents. She understands that time prevented Mrs. Ramsay from creating meaning and intimacy in life, What is the meaning of life...Mrs. Ramsay making of the moment something permanent (as in another sphere Lily herself tried to make of the moment something permanent) this was the nature of a revelation. In the midst of chaos there was shape; this eternal passing and following (she looked at the clouds, going and leaves shaking) was struck in to stability. Life stands still here. Mrs. Ramsay said 'Mrs. Ramsay! Mrs. Ramsay!' She repeated. She owed this revelation to her.(To the Lighthouse, PP.175-6)

Now Lily achieves a moment of community and a sense of unity. Finally, she is able to get rid of her confusions. She is able to achieve the emotional side of Mrs. Ramsay's life. Lily's first inspiration about her painting comes when she thinks about the misguided pity that Mrs. Ramsay has for Mr.

Bankes. She thinks that Mr. Bankes doesn't need this pity because he is a whole and that he is fulfilled in his work.

This reminds her that she, too, has her work. At this moment, she accepts her masculinity. The first revelation comes when she strays herself away from the given gender roles. She has her concept of the ideal femininity and acknowledges that her work is a pursuance of the truth and a rejection of the illusion of the maternally enclosed world.

Lily's acceptance of her work as a masculine and her final assertion of her femininity bring out her vision. She is able to express her mature vision that femininity and masculinity are separate, but equal and personal. Lily draws a line down the middle of her painting. There is a mass on the right which is Mrs. Ramsay and a mass on the left which is Mr. Ramsay. The line down the middle is a divider into equal halves.

She looked at her canvass; it was blurred. With a sudden intensity, as if she saw it clear for a second, she drew a line there, in the centre. It was done; it was finished. Yes she thought, laying down her brush in extreme fatigue, I have had my vision. (To the Lighthouse, P.226)

Mrs. Woolf was one of the great writers whose works reflect her philosophy of life and identification of women. She grew up with an intense interest in the feminist question, and her novels hold the key to the meaning of life and the position of women. In her writing, Woolf makes a sifting appraisal of women's problem, their peculiar dilemmas and conditioning in the traditional Victorian society...Woolf was the most vociferous and vehement on feminist issues such as subjectivity, class, sexuality and culture.

In her critiques, Woolf questions an aesthetic that disallows anger, unreason and passion as productive emotions. Before Woolf's literary works, women's writings were marked by feelings of anger and fear. Woolf bemoaned that women writers' talents were crippled by the authoritarian forces which prevented women from expressing their feelings about the body and mind truthfully.

Woolf believed that it is a part of the occupation of women writers to destroy the patriarchal structures. Woolf strived to give women female identity. In Woolf's strife to set the woman away from the patriarchal society, she called women to re-write the history of women through female eyes and talk about themselves and their experiences truthfully.

Woolf's novels, especially *Mrs. Dalloway* and *To the Lighthouse,* are devoted to portray a picture of a patriarchal and imperialistic society, and to detail the factors that have limited women's opportunities for a meaningful life. In both novels, women suffer alone, have no chances for education, lack warmth and are compelled to suppress their needs.

Virginia Woolf aimed at communicating the message that such a blind social system must be eradicated from its roots. Woolf believed that the oppression of women is rooted in social, economic and psychological factors. Woolf's solution implies the need for self-organization and change in gender identity-different masculinity and femininity. She strived for creating a new man and woman-life, in which both man and woman's identities are realized.

Woolf believed in the distinctiveness of women's values. She argued that these values are compelling reasons for women's participation in public life and necessary to improve the defective social system. She emphasized women's capacity to educate and add a meaningful contribution to our life. It is significant that Woolf chose women characters, not men, to recognize the vision of truth as seen at the end of both novels.

In *Mrs. Dalloway,* Clarissa is able to understand Septimus's vision of reality. Woolf's point is that war can be understood only with reference to the feelings which society considers appropriate only to women. *To the Lighthouse* ends also in a positive feminist note which is seen in Lily's mature vision. By writing *Mrs. Dalloway*, Woolf meant to send an outcry against patriarchy and its representatives. Clarissa moves from one relation to another and every time she is frustrated, and loses the chance to have a happy life with each partner.

Clarissa fails in love and marriage, and misses her chance with sally. Her conventionality, lack of understanding and lack of education are in sharp contrast with Peter's patriarchal demands on woman and his inability to understand her needs. Clarissa rejected Peter's offer of marriage because she prefers privacy to emotion. Entering a marital relationship with Richard, Clarissa is unable to provide him with the kind of relationship usually expected in heterosexual relationships. Clarissa's need for privacy drove her to preserve her virginity, even after having got married to Richard. Richard is excluded from her room, and she gets along with her loneliness and the triviality of her social life.

Woolf always insisted on the importance of women's friendship, and called for a society for women against the oppressive male-dominated society. Clarissa, in her relationship with Sally Seton, sought a society for women. She sought for fulfilling relationship on equal terms. Woolf describes this relationship as 'a protective one'. Clarissa, in her relationship with Sally, broke the authorial voice because bonding with a woman means relationship on equal terms.

Yet both Clarissa and Sally were defeated. They were compelled to ignore their needs because the only accepted female identity was that accepted by patriarchy. Missing the chance with Sally darkens Clarissa's life and fills it with agony. Had she responded to her impulse with Sally Seton, she might have been psychologically fulfilled.

In *Mrs. Dalloway*, the terrible influence of patriarchy is effectively portrayed through the presentation of Miss Kilman and Rezia's lives. Both are victims of the cruelty of the social and political doctrine of the English society and their only guilt is that they are merely women. What is really tragic about Rezia is not her husband's death, but the unfriendly manner in which the world treats her. The cruelty of Miss Kilman's world and her inability to invade the male-dominated teaching profession drove her to deny her femininity and adopt aggressive masculine values. She turns to be a ruthless woman and her life turns to be full of darkness and bitterness.

In *To the Lighthouse*, Woolf makes sharp critical examination of aspects of men-women relationships. Woolf projects the defects of private and public life, and proves that in none of them we can find an adequate model for modern life. The relationship between Mr. and Mrs. Ramsay proves that marriage is not a guarantee of mature and healthy relationship between husband and wife. On one hand, Woolf affirms the femininity of Mrs. Ramsay, but criticizes the way she has chosen to subject her positive feminine traits to male demands.

Lily, unlike Mrs. Ramsay, revolts against masculine needs. She denies her femininity and gets along with self-division in the face of her relationships with men. On the other hand, Woolf discards Mr. Ramsay's masculinity by commenting sarcastically that he has a splendid mind. The tone of the description of his mind is sarcastic because his masculinity is not shown as a positive quality, neither in his relationship with his wife, nor with his children and his work. Mr. Ramsay fails to develop a mature relationship with his wife. He turns into a symbol of tyranny and despotism for his children.

Positive masculinity is to choose methods of fulfillment when the male is able to use his work to be independent and unique, and when he admires and understands the feminine. Had Mr. Ramsay cultivated his femininity and had Mrs. Ramsay had some access to self-fulfilment outside the domestic sphere, they would have held the key for a mature marital relationship.

By writing *Mrs. Dalloway* and *To the Lighthouse,* Mrs. Woolf aimed at setting up a new formula for personal development. She aspired always for the wholeness of personality-androgyny. Androgyny is the blending and balancing of intellect and emotion. It implies that the traditional gender identity, which restricts personal development, can be reformulated through the equal acquisition of the positive feminine and masculine traits.

Woolf introduces women characters who symbolize hope in creating the androgynous world. Elizabeth Dalloway signifies the emergence of the new dawn of women. Thirty years before Elizabeth's age, women couldn't dare to imagine or think of professional life. Elizabeth admires the intelligence of Miss Kilman, and is influenced by her mother more than she realizes.

Woolf suggests that Elizabeth becomes the new woman by uniting her tutor's cleverness and ambitions with her mother's humane sympathies. We find Clarissa that has her own vision in Septimus's death which allows her to face her own misery, step out of the social prison, and have a new vision of life. In comprehending Septimus's death, Clarissa discovers her own identity and becomes a whole.

In *To the Lighthouse,* Woolf rationalizes her quest for the androgynous world through tracing the development of two lines and the coincidence of their triumph at the end of the novel. The completion of lily's picture and the arrival of the Ramsays at the Lighthouse came due to the development of the characters' personalities regarding the truth of their gender. On one hand, Mr. Ramsay tries to fulfil his quest by paying his penance to the memory of his wife, and putting an end to the old enmity with his children.

This can be seen as an improvement of his personality and refinement of his femininity. On the other hand, Lily has the first inspiration about her painting the moment she acknowledges that her work is masculine and also embodies pursuance of truth. At the end of the novel, Lily has a moment of personal wholeness when she accepts the femininity that she has always denied. The novel ends with Lily's vision that femininity and masculinity are separate but equal and personal.

Mrs. Woolf ends *Mrs. Dalloway* and *To the Lighthouse* with two female visions of the truth of our life: Clarissa and Lily's visions. Woolf ends the two novels with a hope for the new woman. Woolf's point is that women shouldn't lose their femininity, and also shouldn't be limited to it, but the woman of the future embraces her femininity and masculinity and makes a choice of how to use that within herself to achieve fulfillment.

Dalit Feminism

In the present scenario "Dalit feminism can be understood through three major streams: struggle of dalit women activists who voiced caste and gender intersectionalities and critiqued the mainstream feminism for being blind to caste; dalit women autobiographers and writer who articulated their authentic experiences of caste and multiple patriarchies; and the theoretical formulation of dalit feminism which has been dominated by a few non-dalit feminist.

The crucial reasons of emerging dalit feminism are ignorance of caste and dalit women's voice in mainstream feminism. Dalit women have formed their different organisations to struggle for their rights and justice in society.

The concept of Dalit feminism, in particular, has been concerned to breakdown the trend of male society; the wide-ranging attitude of male toward women; the harassment and discrimination faced by women and the ways of improving the condition of women and many forth.

The main aim and focus of dalit feminism is dual oppression of number of dalit women on the basis of caste and gender in society. It analyses oppression of dalit women as triple oppression by double patriarchies e.g. discriminative patriarchy of their own caste and overlapping patriarchy of dominant upper castes. Gopal Guru while discussing conditions which make Dalit women a special case argues that Dalit women experience two distinct patriarchal structures/situations: a brahminical form of patriarchy that deeply stigmatized dalit women because of their caste status, as well as the more intimate forms of control by dalit men over the sexual and economic labour.

Brutal patriarchy within so called Dalit communities is one of the central issue which has repeatedly appears in Dalit feminist discourses. Dalit feminism argues that violence of dalit men on their women is sign of their sense of powerlessness in relation to upper castes. In the Hindu dominant Indian society, the violence against dalit women is happen in everyday life.

It is very common that women have second position in society which is the main reason of their subjugation and harassment. The upper caste women also marginalised by the society but difference here between dalit women and upper caste women is that dalit women double marginalised by the society because of her gender and caste. The lower caste women have raised their voice in their writing and depicted all the brutal experience of their own in society. Their resistance against male dominant society can be seen in their own literature known as Dalit Feminist Literature.

The essential theme of the Dalit literature is to emphasize women as victims of sexual exploitation. The women especially Dalit women are molested, raped, assaulted and burnt alive in society for no proper reason. The Dalit literature written by Dalit women have rejected traditional image and have raised their voice against their exploitation. Dalit literature written in particular by dalit women is stentorian because of their sufferings, soreness against caste Hindu, culture and divine laws reflects frequently in dalit women's writing.

The expectation of literature of the dalit feminist is that, each and every women should be honoured and treated as human beings irrespective of their caste. In the dalit feminist writing various themes are very commonly found which are try to make their status equal in society such rebellion, revolt, tortures and sufferings that desire social justice and equality. The dalit feminist writing rejected various bad practices of the society particularly, illiteracy, atrocities, suppression, sexual harassment. They have depicted the real picture of their life in their writings.

In Dalit feminist writing, almost all the protagonists have worked as village servants, cutting woods dragging out dead animals, carrying massages and many such menial works portrayed in large scale in their writing. However, experiences of subjugation, dispossession, segregation, harassment, exploitation and oppression are broadly found in their writing.

The first dalit novel in Tamil is Pazhiyana Kazhidalum written by a dalit woman writer Sivakami and the first dalit autobiography Kurukku by the dalit woman writer Bama who has made her grate contribution in Tamil Dalit Literature. In her 1994 novel Sangati Events Bama portrayed the dual oppression of women by virtue of sexual orientation and position. "Sangati is a women's activist account wherein Bama attempts to grow women's activist motivation to enroll rank persecution as a subject of concern.

The writing of Bama and her Novel Sangati Events celebrates the lives of dalit women of her community. She has brought the predicament of dalit women front of the society through her writings. The novel is full of terrific stories of the dalit families of her village. She has used confessional mode of narration in her Sangati Events. The depiction of the Dalit women is an essential facet of Tamil Dalit Literature in terms of space and voice granted to Dalit women characters. In Dalit literature and particularly in Tamil Dalit literature women characters of the Dalit background are represented as lively, vibrant, earthly, witty, hardworking women who have personal power to face crisis and work at private sphere and public sphere. Their dances, songs, community cooking at wedding bring out their native talent.

The most of the Dalit writers are use the revolutionary language in their writing. The use of abuse word as commonly used among the people and the real presentation of society is the actuality of Dalit literature. In Sangati Events Bama has portrayed the life of women in both private and public sphere and has presented brutal cruelties of male centric society. Her Dalit women characters are faced many difficulties in their own houses and outside the houses and village. She has criticised double patriarchy of dalit women in her novel. When Marriamma was in field for firewood, she has attacked by upper caste man for his sexual fulfilment but she escaped from his hand and reach at home. She save her honour from upper caste man but front of her community she was not able to protect it. The man who has attacked Marriamma in the field complaint that he has saw Marriamma and Mannikam was behaving in dirty way.

The head and people of the community have believed in his story and punished both innocent Marriamma and Mannikam in front of the community. It is very common in dalit communities in India. Marriamma has humiliated and exploited in such way that she wish to destroyed herself. There were many women watching Marriamma's predicament but know one dare to utter a single word to protect her humiliation. Patti a central character dug out the reason of this muteness of women.

There are different kinds of atrocities committed on dalit women in public sphere which are captured in Bama's Sangati Events in details. Except of public sphere the exploitation and predicament of women is also not good in private sphere, it means women also have faced many difficulties even in their own homes. Bama has satirized the predicament of women by their own husbands. In her community women have no rights to go against men.

The women in both the spheres are not treated equally by the male dominant society. In Sangati Events Bama reproduces the diminished and violent world of dalit women. Dalit women characters of Bama suffer from double discrimination and marginalisation. They are oppressed by the upper caste people and also by dalit males, even dalit women treated as other in male dominant society. The horrible patriarchal differences are begins to introduce in children within the early ten years of their lives. There are different types of games based on gender, it means the game of male are not for women or women not allowed to play such game.

Bama in her early age as young girl familiar with the crafty nature of gender games they play. In her community girls are not allowed to play the games of boys which has created disparities between male and female and made them other in society. She has clearly mentioned that games like Kabbadi and Marbles are meant for boys in which women suppose to not participate either they have will or not. They are only forcefully play at home different games such as cooking, getting married and other various domestic tasks against their will.

Her novel is full of such stories which has depicted the place of women in society. As dalit writer and the witness of all those unequal things in society for dalit women Bama criticised this kind of unjust did of the male and especially dalit male. It is clear that the notion of women or dalit women as other is based almost exclusively on the notion of sexual differences which is crucially described in Bama's Sangati Events.

The central focus of the dalit literature is the depiction of various issues of exploitation, discrimination, starvation and growing rate death of the neglected sections of Indian society such as untouchable minorities, nomadic tribes, the tribals and other inferior lives.. In her Sangati Events Bama has depicted such kind of different issues of the society which women are facing from long period. The novel clears Bama's resistance to society in different event and her different characters.

The women of the dalit community treated very badly at the field by their landowner as well as by their husbands at home. The dalit men who have no rights to expressed their words front of the upper caste people, although these dalit people wants more freedom from their wives and do control on them. In Sangati Events Bama resist such event and suggest, "we must be strong. We must show by our own resolute lives that we believe ardently in our independence... we must never allow our minds to be worn out, damaged, and broken in the belief that this is our fate. Just as we work hard so long as there is strength in our bodies, so too, must we strengthen our hearts and minds in order to survive" (59).

Bama very powerfully narrates her stories and try to unite and make familiar women about their rights. She shows her resistance to various bad practices of the society is not well enough for the dalit women. She has created consciousness and awareness among dalit women. She realizes that such sort of blind belief and self-submission can be removed only by the collective action. Dr.B.R. Ambedkar was greatest radical thinker of the Indian society who has shown the real path to so called untouchable community across India.

The whole Dalit literature is inspire from Ambedkar and Bama too not exception of it. In her community, people are gathered for Ambedkar talked for social consciousness and awareness however, people from the upper caste treated badly with dalits after such talked and used abuse word for women. She says, when "Our boys are going around everywhere talking about Ambedkar. But it really only causes trouble for us. When we tried to go to work, the landlords wouldn't let us work for him, but drove us away, saying, "You people had better go and make living by working on your great Ambedkar's fields. Why come here?" (103). Here is much more need to change this kind of attitude of the upper caste people who behave badly with dalit men and women because of their talked on Ambedkar.

This is not only in short range to Bama's community but also all the socially and economically suppressed and depressed communities of India. The dalit women are facing different kind of discrimination in their daily lives. There are various reasons to predicament of women in society. They are tolerating those entire things which are imposed by male dominant society. Bama boldly express her views and suggests women to stop this kind of inequality in society.

The novel Sangati Events is an account on Bama's community and testimonio of the predicament of dalit women. To recapitulate, Bama in the whole novel has been depicted various issues of women which are creating disparities between men and women. Caste is the very significant observable fact in the novel which is enough to show brutality and exploitation of the women by upper caste people in the society.

The novel Sangati is enough to increased voice of women against atrocities, and it also demand equal rights to women, particularly dalit women who kept away from the mainstream feminism. The establishment of equality among gender is not easy task in Indian society because of mindset of male for rule over female. Thus, notion of gender is the real villain and has to be demolished from the society, because it is nothing real but social construction. The central, radical and essential focus of dalit feminism is the unjust discrimination between men and women.

BLACK FEMINISM

Chimamanda Ngozi Adichie was born on 15th September 1977 at Enugu, Eastern Nigeria. She grew up in the university town of Nsukka which is the fictional town in her works. Adichie"s two novels explore the complexities of human experience inspired by social and political events in her native Nigeria. Her first novel Purple Hibiscus, which explores patriarchy, domestic violence, religious fundamentalism and general intolerance, was published in October 2003 receiving extensive international acclaim.

It won Huston/Wright legacy award in 2004 and was short-listed for Orange Broadband Prize for Fiction. Later it was awarded the Common wealth Prize for the Best First Fiction Book 2005.

Her short story „Half of a Yellow Sun" won the PEN/David Wong short story award in 2003 and she expanded it to her second novel, Half of a Yellow Sun (2006). Her story is built on the themes of colonialism, neocolonialism, tribalism, corruption, love, marriage and domestic (dis) unity in the background of the Biafra war. This novel won the Orange Broadband Prize for Fiction 2007. Her anthology of short stories, The Thing Around Your Neck, was published in 2009. Adichie is the latest Nigerian female writer to make a mark in the African literary scene and to win several international prizes within a short time. She is quoted to have said that her greatest inspiration comes from Chinua Achebe.

Many African female writers like Nwapa (1966), Emecheta (1981), Dangaremgba (1988), Mugo (1988) and Aidoo (1977) among others have written stories seeking to expunge women"s marginal position(s) and thus their texts are „spaces of strength within and between which they fluctuate as opined by Nfah-Abbenyi (1997). In line with this, D'Almeida (1994) considers writing by women as a weapon to destroy the ideas that perpetuate subjugation and inequality.

Most literary scholars dealing with African literature such as Stratton (1994), Steady(1998), Ogundipe-Leslie(1987), Emenyonu(2004), Oyeronke (2009) agree that works by African women writers are rarely discussed and seldom accorded space in canon formation thus making much of the African literature appear male-centred. This makes Leek (1999) argue that African women have been indoctrinated to envision the world from a patriarchal perspective.

An African woman is to be totally deprived of equality and thus African female writers have taken responsibility of redressing this mistake and re-defining the meaning of being an African woman. In doing so, women writers have tried to look for a possible centre in the periphery of female imagination. In our reading and interpretation of Adichie"s two novels we explore how she struggles to give African women a proper place with dignity denied by patriarchy and other forms of subjugation.

In contemporary writing, African women wrestle with those problems that confront women and also shape the continent.

According to Ogundipe-Leslie (1994), African feminism should endeavour to empower women and society and thus sexual politics is intricately intertwined with other struggles in the continent. Generally speaking then, the apparent concern of an African writer, male or female, is to speak about immediate issues or concerns of social life.

This is because Africa has a distinct condition occasioned by its history as argued by Amuta (1989), that: African literature and its criticism testify the historical contradictions that define the African situation. In order to resolve these contradictions in the direction of progressive change, literary criticism must be predicated on a theoretical outlook that couples cultural theory back to social practice. In this respect, literary theory and practice must form part of anti-imperialist struggle thus demystifying literary criticism and reintegrating it into the social experience and practice of which literature itself is very much part.

Amuta seems to suggest that literature should be part of the neo-colonial struggle in the African context where the process of emancipation is not yet over. The African man, like the African woman, is a victim of different forms of oppression; dictatorship, racism, poverty, ethnicity and neo-colonialism among others. Our study thus, interrogates the oppression of the African women as depicted in the context of other African problems as Adichie highlights them in her two works.

African women scholars like Emecheta (1981), Kolawole (1997), Badejo (1999) and Ogunyemi (1985) have disowned and rejected the label „feminism" as they explore women"s voicelessness and/or (in) audibility and human oppression in their writings. They have accused Western feminism of universalizing women's experience and hence occasioning cultural imperialism. Said (1993) confirms that Third World societies are designated in exclusionary terms and so women are excluded lot from most discourses even those that concern them. Min-Ha (1989) holds the same view when he argues that third world women are treated as an out-group to be spoken for by mainstream in-group. This leads us to the big question posed by Spivak (1999),

The desire for self-naming reflects the rights to self-validation, thus the quest by African women to name their experiences, map their strategies for struggle and the realisation of true liberation for African men and women. African women have rejected being named by outsiders because such are alien labels. Western women have named and defined the African woman within Eurocentric perspectives, disregarding her socio-cultural and political milieu. Women empowerment through self-definition and self-naming in the African situation enables women to cope and transcend their oppression.

Argued this way, African women writers like Adichie are therefore Womanists and not feminists as pointed out by Ogunyemi (1985) and Kolawole (1997). This study is in line with the insights of Steady (1998), Kolawole (1997) and Badejo (1999) who argue that gender roles in Africa are complementary, similar, asymmetrical and automatically linked to continuity of life in the continent. Thus, it is true that a feminist movement confined to specific oppression of women cannot, in isolation end exploitation and imperialism.

The submissions of Hander (1999) are quite relevant to this study since she argues that women have broken rules of race and gender in order to embody hope for the future of the nation. This means that women are integral in building a new African society, stressing the damaging effect of subjugation outside the colonizer-colonized relationship. We read Adichie as an African woman writer and pay special attention to how she engages in creating oppositional discourse to bring to light human suffering and the humiliation suffered by women and the African people.

Adichie becomes the voice of her people and her generation by crafting fictional stories aimed at subverting oppressive structures in her society. This is because African women writers have to create stories that are tellingly appropriate and instructive as their first concern as they struggle with women oppression and innumerable problems that bedevil the continent.

Ogunyemi (1985) contends that African female writers should not be limited to issues defined by their femaleness but should attempt to tackle questions raised by their humanity. The way African women partner with their men to fight oppression is an outstanding component of our study. We can therefore argue that an African woman writer should not just bridge the gap between Western and African thought but create something new out of both with the aim of challenging the tradition which appears to ignore or trivialize either black (African) or female concerns.

Purple Hibiscus is Adichie"s first novel and one of its major themes is domestic violence. Women have always been on the receiving end when it comes to domestic violence and through the character of Beatrice this novel explores how wives are subjugated by their husbands. Beatrice's world is exclusively controlled by her husband. She is not entitled to any choice and feelings of her own. One occurrence that confirms this is when the family visits Father Benedict after a Sunday service.

Papa's word is final and he disregards the wife's feelings and thus Beatrice hangs at the periphery of Papa's world. Despite being unwell she is compelled to go with the rest to the priest's house. At home, she has no choice over what colour of curtains to hang on the windows of the family mansion. The indecision depicted here confirms the marginal position Beatrice occupies in relation to her husband. Beatrice struggles from the periphery and emerges as the pro-active character who decapitates patriarchy (by poisoning the husband) and that way moves to the centre where she is autonomous to make her own choices.

The suffering that Beatrice goes through can only be eased by removing Eugene out of her space and so the writer's act is the final act of tearing down patriarchy and its attendant violence. It does not mean destroying men since Beatrice desires to have a loving man in her life. Eugene's attack of his pregnant wife is not only a manifestation of the evil face of patriarchy but also the insensitivity of such practice to basic principles of humanity.

His personality is well described by Hewett (2004) as a strict catholic who lives within the Manichean dictates of unforgiving faith." Mama"s act of raising her hands while being flogged together with her children (102) is symbolic of surrender and helplessness that grip women once exposed to male violence. The author condemns Mama"s failure to speak about her situation since the silence re-energizes Eugene resulting to several misfortunes that would have been averted.

Although Mama is abused and unloved, she is subservient to her husband as expected in her marriage. She can only respond to her predicament by crying. Kambili observes that: She cried for a long time. She cried until her hand, clasped in hers, felt stiff. She cried until Aunty Ifeoma finished cooking the rotting meat in a spicy stew. She cried until she fell asleep, her head against the seat of the chair. Jaja laid her on a mattress on the living room floor (249).

Crying makes Mama"s situation starkly hopeless and irredeemable. As readers we pity Mama and sympathize with the anguish she is going through. Mama cries in the face of violence and when Kambili is hospitalized after being assaulted by Papa she observes from her hospital bed that: Mama reached out to hold my hand. Her face was puffy from crying, and her lips were cracked, with bits of discoloured skin peeling off. I wished I could get up and hug her and yet I wanted to push her away, to shove her so hard that she would topple over the chair (213).

The feelings afflicting Kambili in this episode are due to the indifference that Mama has exhibited over time in regard to Papa"s violence. Kambili wishes that Mama could do something. At St Agnes hospital Mama cries out of the love she has for her injured daughter. She acts in a similar manner when Papa scalds the feet of his children for sharing a house with their grandfather in Nsukka. African women are therefore seen as helpless but sympathetic to their daughters' suffering as is the case with Beatrice in Purple Hibiscus.

Mother'S sympathy comes from within their souls since they closely identify with their daughters because one day the daughters will grow to be mothers/women. Adichie depicts women as sympathetic to their situation. However, she disparages Mama"s silence and inaction and suggests that women should shout their oppression in an effort to confront the conscience of their oppressors. To Beatrice a husband coronets woman"s life and she cannot quit the marriage despite the prodding from Ifeoma.

In Purple Hibiscus Adichie uses the character of Beatrice to encourage women to react to oppression since remaining passive gives the oppressor some impetus to repeat his behaviour. The opening lines of Purple Hibiscus signal a threat to continued co-existence of the family members because of lack of free space. The home is in turmoil and things are about to fall apart. It means the centre symbolised by the paternal authority cannot hold anymore and further suggests that several centres of authority are necessary. It is in the other centre(s) where the characters living in Eugene"s family enjoy freedom.

Kambili is concerned about every member of the family but does not speak her mind because of „lack of freedom to be, to say" (16). Mama informs the daughter that she will not replace the figurines and Kambili realises that, „when Papa threw the missal at Jaja it was not just the figurines that came tumbling down, it was everything" (15). Everything" implies even the authority that Papa has over his family. Mama"s refusal to replace the figurines suggests a need to live without the usual patriarchal control occasioned by Eugene.

Religion is partly to blame for what Papa becomes since he is brought up by a priest and as a result his world is structured in Biblical terms of evil versus righteousness. The familial space, occupied by Beatrice and her children is so packed with catholic rituals and religious activities that they have no time left for anything else. However, this constriction of people"s freedom dictated by religion exists only at St Agnes in Enugu and not anywhere else. At Nsukka the church accords its members some liberties and that way religion is a source of freedom and not a burden to the faithful.

The church at Enugu knows the happenings at Eugene's house but does nothing to rectify the mess. Because God is love as per the inscriptions on Mama"s T-shirt, the church is ridiculed by Adichie when it fails to preach the same love to wife batterers like Eugene. Father Benedict becomes one of the contemptible priests in the novel in sharp contrast with Father Amadi. Adichie pours scorn on any kind of faith that encourages oppression. She calls on her people to snub those churches which do not do anything to expand democratic space or entrench equity among the faithful.

Mama's duties attract fewer benefits than those of her husband who is always meeting business people, government officials and his Standard editor to discuss seemingly very important national issues.

Mama's influence is limited to the domestic space whereas that of Papa is the public space (international) since Amnesty World gives him an award for speaking against oppression. The irony of this award is evident when Eugene does not accord the slightest freedom to his immediate family members.

In this episode Adichie attacks the patriarchal order that purports to support and speak for women but oppresses them instead. Everyone at Eugene"s family exhibits peculiar apprehension occasioned by Papa"s religiosity and ritualized living. Eugene"s ghost dangles precariously threatening other family members in their private lives. The narrator feels suffocated and the framed photos of the grandfather bear down upon her. Any symbol of male authority becomes a burden and Kambili happens to see this in all those things that Papa stands for like his religion.

Therefore the portrait of Kambili's maternal grandfather becomes one of the symbols of the suppressive patriarchal order in place. Hot tea, given to Kambili by Papa in the name of love sip is a source of torment to the young narrator: The tea was always too hot, always burned my tongue and if lunch was something peppery, my raw tongue suffered. But it didn't matter because I knew that when the tea burned my tongue, it burned Papa's love into me (8). This kind of punishment that Kambili suffers yet cannot complain about serves to explain how patriarchy manifests itself and destroys those who it is meant to shelter.

The hot tea experience points to the contradictions in Papa's house. Eugene"s family is housed in an enclosed compound where dealing with the outside world is completely curtailed. High walls topped with electric wires contain anything from either going out or coming in. This ensures that the violence that the family suffers is not known to the outside world. It also prevents new and liberatory ideas from filtering in. They are very much held in a controlled domestic space thus they depend on Papa"s knowledge and ideas over everything.

It can be argued that patriarchy has always tried to control the domestic space and deny women the chance to enter into the public sphere symbolised by the Eugene's family compound. Mama, a symbol of oppressed African women, suffers such suppressing internment. She has no voice and does not talk to Papa; she is a dehumanized wife and suffers in solitary. Adichie"s texts therefore seem to prod women to identify and challenge structures of patriarchal exclusion which possibly serve to deny them vital knowledge for their emancipation.

In an effort to voice prejudice in gender relations, polygamy is vilified in Purple Hibiscus through the character of Ezendu's second wife. She is said to have driven out the senior wife. It is from the spitefulness of such practice that mother and daughter applaud Papa for not taking a second wife despite encouragement from the clan to do so. What we discover from Beatrice and Kambili's discussion can be construed to mean that marital comfort for most women in polygamous set ups is never realised. What polygamy does is to isolate women, control their sexuality and promote patriarchy.

In highlighting this Adichie disparages polygamy and opens it for social ridicule. Yewande Cocker weeps for her husband when he is arrested and wonders how she would manage to sustain the family alone. But as Yewande cries out for the simple arrest, Aunty Ifeoma"s husband is dead and she manages her family single-handed. Adichie, in these events is suggesting that women can make a living without husbands (men) and still be prosperous and happy.

The desire for a good man to complement a woman's life is however hinted at when Beatrice strongly talks of the need of a man in a woman"s life. It is such a need for a loving companion that makes Yewande cry. It can therefore be argued that Adichie proposes that women should live a happy married life but where situations do not work they should strive to make their life livable without men. Marriage makes women proud and the way

Ifeoma's student keeps calling the fiancée *'dim'*, my husband" pinpoints to the way courting and marriage presents women with multiple positive possibilities.

Ifeoma, however, has different perceptions regarding marriage. She harbors feelings close to bitterness when her students move to marry at a young age. To her, marriage suffocates the numerous chances for women and makes them live like Beatrice, her sister-in-law. The family consequently becomes a site of oppression for women. Adichie highlights a situation where married wives belong to the extended family and that is why Aunty Ifeoma calls Beatrice my wife. The family then becomes a source of power for the daughters who own their brothers" wives but elsewhere the family appears to disempower and subordinate the married women.

Aunty Ifeoma is supposed to take the children to the late husband's hometown even though she complains that Ifediora's *umunna* is not treating her well. Mama informs aunty that the boys should get to know their *umunna* a thinking which places boys and generally men at a position above girls and women. The demand made by Beatrice that Ifeoma should take her children to their hometown shows how children tie married women to their husband"s clan. Ifeoma is reluctant about taking the children to Ifediora's hometown and that way serves as a symbol of the rebellious modern woman who will eschew patriarchy.

Ifeoma challenges the way the government appoints university administrators. She is thereafter accused of being disloyal and is subjected to police harassment, sacked and finally forced to go into exile. It is from exile where her daughter Amaka writes home to condemn the Nigerian justice system. Ifeoma and Amaka can therefore be read as Adichie's schema aimed at suggesting ways of emancipating the African women from the yoke of patriarchy and other forms of exploitation.

Aunty Ifeoma brings up her children teaching them how to do all sorts of household tasks. She does not discriminate against the children on gender lines especially when assigning domestic duties. Adichie appears to challenge society to bridge the chasm in the socialization process where boys are treated differently from girls. The experience that Eugene's children have at aunty Ifeoma"s house in Nsukka leads to a revolution.

There is increased consciousness and desire for freedom at the domestic front as Jaja and Kambili head home from Nsukka. Jaja demands to have the key to his room and Kambili notes: I wanted to tell Mama that it did feel different to be back, that our living room had too much empty space, too much wasted marble floor that gleamed from Sisi's polishing and housed nothing. Our ceilings were too high. Our furniture was lifeless: the glass tables did not shed twisted skin in the harmattan, the leather sofas" greeting was a clammy coldness, the Persian rugs were too lush to have any feeling (192).

A considerable change in thinking and looking at the world has taken place because of the visit to Nsukka"s. Kambili is able to identify the high goals Papa sets for them contrary to Nsukka where Ifeoma allows the cousins to explore and scale their heights. Through the journeying motif Kambili discovers her true self and her desire for freedom is heightened.

The cousins have a voice to speak their joys, aspirations, sorrows and to explain their world, which are the things Jaja and Kambili miss at Enugu. Silence in Eugene's house is perverse but there is a lot of talk, laughter, singing and exchange at Aunty Ifeoma"s house.

In superimposing the two environments Adichie advocates for upbringing like that of Ifeoma where girls are not discriminated from boys and domestic chores are shared equally regardless of gender. The home, according to Adichie should be a garden where different flowers bloom like Ifeoma"s garden. Exaggerated religious rituals are also not very common in Nsukka as they happen to be in Enugu. Amaka has to choose a confirmation name and has insists on an African name but Kambili has Papa pick the name Ruth for her.

The author pairs the two families to suggest an alternative upbringing and gender socialization. When Eugene attacks Kambili with kicks and blows, Mama stands aside and pleads please *biko*!" (211). Mama unconsciously approves Papa's way of doing things thus presents submissiveness, piety and domesticity equivalent to Okonkwo's wives in Achebe's Things Fall Apart (1958) who stand aside as Okonkwo beats their co-wife Ojiugo.

Mama's action also maps to what Maiguru does when Babamukuru assaults Nyasha in Dangarembga's Nervous Conditions (1988). Such behaviour from married women shows how patriarchy compels women to comply with its ideology through the use of violence. Adichie suggests that women should do something to change how society functions through the character of Ifeoma.

Ifeoma is angry about oppression and lack of freedom at both domestic and public levels. It is the disturbing helplessness and passivity that she finds with Beatrice and some colleagues at the university that Adichie admonishes. Adichie"s voice calls upon women to identify all forms of social oppression and to go ahead and confront the same. After Papa's death and Jaja's incarceration Mama and Kambili take over the management of the family and the family finances. They even get to know who to bribe, to hire or to fire.

Though they are silent it is silence with freedom. They have their own voice and when Mama turns to Kambili and says Thank you Kambili tells us. It is one of the few times in the past three years that she has spoken without first being spoken to (306). This is an indication of a new family that has freedom and some joy though it has its problems and ghosts. Although Papa is dead, Jaja as a son and brother is ready to suffer on behalf of the mother and sister. Through Jaja, Adichie suggests masculine selflessness and a regard for women.

Wives are expected to be mothers and motherhood has over time been seen as a source of strength in most African communities. All over the world women have had status and respect for their role in nurturing and ensuring continuity. Freud (1963) describes the mother as the child's primary love object and the parent most responsible for its optimal development. He argues that in the early years of an infant's life the relationship of the infant with the mother is close but during the Oedipal conflict the boy renounces the love of his mother in fear of his more powerful father.

Freud further affirms that the girl moves away from her mother who she sees as powerless and castrated. Motherhood is highly valued among the Mende people who according to Kolawole (1997) worshiped wives for being bringers of life. Kolawole however, argues that women have over time been excluded from vital areas of decision making in the public arena. According to Oyewumi (2001) motherhood is a defining feature for African women but for this study, we investigate how it is a possible source of exploitation, oppression and exclusion within the social-political space in Purple Hibiscus.

Purple Hibiscus surveys motherhood through the characters of Beatrice and Aunty Ifeoma. De Beauvoir (1989) argues that women's ability to give birth is subsequently the source of their subordination. She contents that motherhood signals that women were twice doomed: biologically during pregnancy and socially when children restricted them at home. Chodorow (1978) blames sexual inequality in society on the division of labour that allocates the primary infant and child care to women at home while men take valued occupations outside.

She further posits that in most society's daughters and sons are treated differently and consequently developed differently. The daughters who share the core female identity with the mother copy their mother while the sons remain separate and autonomous. The societal desire for children happens to be an avenue through which women are exploited and oppressed. Linked with the desire for children is also the strong social demand and desire to mother boys.

Due to the high premium attached to boy-child girls inhabit second position and that leads to their degradation. This desire for babies makes Beatrice in Purple Hibiscus struggle desperately to meet the *umunna's* expectations of *omelora's* (an Igbo elder) wife. The members of Eugene"s *umunna* are opposed to his having two children only. Beatrice spends much of her time attending to domestic duties mainly on behalf of her children and the husband.

Immediately Papa throws the missal to Jaja and breaks the figurines it is Mama who picks them with bare hands since it is risky for the family members if they remain strewn there. Jaja warns Mama „careful, Mama, or those pieces will cut your fingers (8) This is a confession from the son that

Mama would do anything to make sure the family is safe. Mama plaits the hair of Kambili every Sunday before lunch.

While Beatrice [mama] does most of the domestic duties after Sunday, Papa enjoys his siesta. This highlights an uneven situation for men and women. Mama's obligations place her squarely in the domestic arena. It is no surprise that when Aunty Ifeoma wants to take them out Mama cannot go because she tells Ifeoma that, „you know Eugene likes me to stay around (80)." Therefore, the domestic space, reserved for mothers, is a site of patriarchal oppression.

The characters and circumstances in Purple Hibiscus compare well with Dangarembga's Nervous Conditions (1988) where Eugene just like Babamukuru are symbols of masculinity. Both are domineering, benevolent and they provide for their own families and the clan but are callous, unreasonable, brutal and oppressive. Despite these men being highly educated they exploit their wives and Just like Beatrice in Purple Hibiscus, Maiguru in Nervous Conditions has to lie low and to continuously pamper Babamukuru.

The attitude towards women and girls does not change whether the men are educated or not since Eugene is well educated and so is Babamukuru. Adichie seems to suggest that negative patriarchy rears its ugly face in Africa in the modern era despite the progress made in different areas of human endeavour. It means that women can only be respected if they fulfill their biological duty of mothering. Mama fears Papa may marry other women who may give Papa more sons and displace her.

For a woman to have security and a permanent position then she should have several children and more so boys.

The experiences of Beatrice are reminiscent of what Nnu Ego in Emecheta"s The Joys of Motherhood (1979) goes through as she struggles to prove herself as a mother. Such a demand is pegged on African women"s need to be disparaged or at least revised to give women a breathing space as hinted to by Adichie. Although Aunty Ifeoma is educated and enjoys more freedom than Beatrice, she is also held by her family such that she spends much of her time with the children: helping, correcting, punishing, encouraging and cooking. She is widowed and struggling as Papa-Nnukwu realizes. Since the father of her children died, she has seen hard times" (65).

Kambili notes that she behaves like a referee who has done a good job and admires to watch the players who in this case are her children: Amaka, Obiora and Chima. Adichie uses Ifeoma's character to open women's eyes to the realities of patriarchy and also to suggest alternative avenues to self-actualization. She stands against oppression when everyone else is silent. Through this character Adichie pronounces her convictions that the oppressed should constantly challenge their oppressor.

The identity of women is linked to their children and we realise that those women who are childless suffer the indignity of lacking mother derived identity. This is realised in Ogige Market where Kambili notes: Mama Joe's shed in Ogige Market just barely fit the high stool where she sat and the smaller stool in front of her...Women and children worked in the neighboring sheds, twisting hair, weaving hair, plaiting hair with thread. Wooden boards with lopsided print leaned on broken chairs in front of the sheds.

From this extract we realize the identity of mothers is crucial in getting business names. Such identification serves to marginalize those who are childless. Rarely have women been studied as daughters in literature since the identity of wives and mothers overshadow other identities. This happens despite the affirmations of Oyewumi (1997) that seniority; to be precise older/young is more important than sex/gender in African context. She further points out that sex/gender are absolute: one is either a man or a woman or is not (for the transsexuals) yet seniority is relational; one is young or older depending on the context and situation.

Seniority unlike gender is only graspable as part of relationships and neither rigidly fixated on the body nor dichotomized. These insights are critical as we try to make sense of the identity of women as daughters which is an identity in transition in the worlds of the two novels. In Purple Hibiscus, the socialization of daughters produces docile, submissive and unimaginative characters due to the oppressive and overly patriarchal environment they grow up in.

To Papa, Kambili should be God fearing and a backyard snob as the girls in her class point out. She simply does things in a weird way; isolating herself from the other students and remaining silent. Okuyade (2007) affirms that silence in Purple Hibiscus is magnified to a level whereby it can be heard.

Kambili, Jaja and their mother are so oppressed that they speak with their spirits. In a rare twist Mama kills her husband and that way frees herself and her children from the yoke of domestic servitude. This killing is symbolic in that it points to the author"s desire of a world free of gender engineered violence at the domestic level. The Biblical allusion of Jesus serves to exonerate Mama from the killing since Jaja and Kambili believe that someone has to die for some other people to be saved.

Kambili says: God knows best, I said. God works in mysterious ways." And I thought how Papa would be proud that I had said that...Look what He did to his faithful servant Job, even to His own son. But have you ever wondered why? Why did He have to murder his own son so we would be saved? Why did He have to go ahead and save us? (289). For the freedom of women to be fully realized sometimes drastic and radical measures have to be taken.

Adichie, in her second novel half of a Yellow Sun tackles issues which are thematically related to what is in Purple Hibiscus. The author projects women characters struggling to keep their families hopeful even when the country is going through a civil war. In half of a Yellow Sun women are depicted as resolute and progressive. They give direction when and where necessary and guide their men and society in time of difficulties. Those women who are not progressive are drawn in the negative light and we, as readers, are called upon to disregard them.

Adichie uses characters like Alice to state her position on mistresses, concubinage and being second wives. Alice is depicted as eccentric and anti-social. She is always sheepishly taking herself to very unfulfilling male relationships. Even though she complains of the army officer who dupes her we are quite unhappy when she lures Odenigbo while Olanna is at Orlu. Adichie uses the character of Alice to rebuke women who betray other women in infidelity or in polygamy.

Infidelity on the part of men is a serious challenge women have to often grapple with in Half of a Yellow sun. Mrs Ozobia is a victim of negative masculinity since her husband has a mistress, a Yoruba woman for whom he has bought a house in a neighborhood where Lagos socialites live. The desire for children is explored through the characters of Olanna, Arize, Odenigbo"s mother and Anulika among others in Half of a Yellow Sun. It is the desire for a child and a grandson that drives Odenigbo's mother to coerce Amala into sleeping with Odenigbo and this leads to the near collapse of Odenigbo"s relationship with Olanna. To Mama Odenigbo, a spoiled woman is one who cannot bear children. She says, No-body knows if she can have children. Do you know? Does anyone know?" (198).

Mama"s concern grows out of the significance attached to children in Igbo society and by extension Africa. She seriously wants to have a grandson. She complains that those girls who go to University follow men until their bodies are useless to have children. She says no wonder my son has not married while his mates are counting how many children they have" (97). The situation described here resembles what happens in Nwapa's One is Enough (1990) where Amaka"s relationship with her husband Obiora is strained by mother-in-law who accuses her of being barren.

We can therefore conclude that childlessness is apparently a permanent source of frustration to the African women as portrayed in the above cited examples. Children take care of parents and carry on the family name. This explains why women and society are controlled by the desire to have many children so as to carry the family name and enlarge the husband's *umunna*. This in itself point to the patriarchal nature of Adichie's society that ties a woman to the husbands *umunna* by virtue of having mothered boys.

In an effort to bring about change in the institution of motherhood, adoption is suggested as a more progressive way to tackle childlessness. Olanna adopts Amala"s child and cares for her because the mother rejects her immediately she is born. The same happens with Mrs Ozobia in that Aunty Ifeka nursed Olanna and Kainene because her breasts dried soon after they were born. As a result, Olanna thinks that Aunty Ifeka was as good as her mother. It is Aunty Ifeka that Olanna runs to when she has problems with Odenigbo.

Olanna also feels glad when the nurse asks her how many children she has. Her feelings emanate out of what society demands from women: motherhood. A similar societal obsession with the desire to have children is what makes Arize's mother-in-law disgrace her by demanding to know how many abortions she has had before marriage. Nnakwanze also is worried when Arize does not become pregnant the first, second and third year of their marriage. Arize's misfortune is a source of oppression from her mother-in-law.

It is what Amala suffers in the hands of Odenigbo's mother, in that Odenigbo"s mother wants to use her to get a grandson. Such a situation puts women under a lot of pressure, curtails their freedom and makes them slaves of societal demand(s) and desire(s) leaving them without a choice of their own.

The characters of the old women (mother-in-law) in the text shows that patriarchy has conditioned women to accept demands put across by the male order. In accepting the patriarchal demands and forcing fellow women to follow suit they have become perpetrators of their own suffering. Through the characters of Ifeoma, Olanna and Kainene, Adichie shows that motherhood can be revised in order to stop women oppression and suffering. In the use of Kainene and Olanna Adichie revises the perception that women should have on issues of motherhood.

Whatever is captured in Half of a Yellow Sun in terms of women and motherhood is progressive unlike what we get in Purple Hibiscus. Kainene and Olanna do not value motherhood so much and Kainene remains in her relationship without a child for the entire life of the novel. Olanna adopts Amala"s child. Kainene and Richard are happy and prosperous despite childlessness. This is the world that Adichie proposes whereby women are less burdened by their biological duties of mothering.

In Half of a Yellow Sun Adichie depicts daughters who reject to be tools of male aggrandizement through the episode where Ozobia uses his daughter Olanna to get a contract from the Minister of Finance; chief Okonji. Olanna is uncomfortable about it: She wondered, too, how her parents had promised chief Okonji an affair with her in exchange for the contract. ou as sex bait,"... (35).

This demonstrates the use of women by men in the society represented by Adichie for material gains. When the parents conspire to have Olanna get sexually involved with the finance minister they paint an ugly picture of daughters who have no choice of even sexual partners. We learn that Olanna's father did not receive her choice of Odenigbo positively. The narrator identifies that all is not well with Odenigbo as Olanna's fiancée and notes, her father only wanted to gall him and show how unimpressed he was by a senior lecturer from Nsukka (32). Such wish of parents to control Olanna's choice of partners is explored when Olanna talks about her mother and the different opinions they hold over her choices.

Adichie brings up a situation where Olanna rebels to suggest that women should stand their grounds on issues of personal choice. Personal choice points to characters autonomy and some degree of liberty on the part of women. Eberechi suffers during the war in that she is used as sex bait and denied her right to choose a partner. Such an act is a total disregard of her humanity and denies the young girl her basic rights.

Adichie highlights these episodes to herald positive change for the betterment of women's welfare. In comodifying daughters, Adichie is condemning the difference of being the owner of property, the heir (for boys and men) and being the property (for daughters and women) and thus suggesting a revision to the existing gender parities.

Adichie in Half of a Yellow Sun sees women as progressive elements in society in the sense that they are the promoters of their society during very trying times like during the Biafra War. Women desperately and continuously search for food and medicine during the war and that way sustain their communities. Kainene introduces the idea of growing crops to feed the refugees during the time when there is no food forthcoming to the Biafrans. Olanna goes ahead to try and get an alternative job for her husband who appears withdrawn as the war presses forward. She also starts a school to teach the children such that there would be continuity after the war.

Adichie satirizes the activities of *umunna* which is a male caucus for enslaving women. Women are totally against what *umunna* does or says since it is an institution that serves to marginalize them. Members of Ifediora's *umunna* say a lot of negative things about Ifeoma. And as mentioned earlier in Eugene"s *umunna* advices him to take a second wife so that he could have children since a man of his stature cannot take pride in only two children. Cultures are mostly created by men and that is why most of them are oppressive to women making them act within male confines.

Bride-price, polygamy, picking partners for sons/daughters, desire for children and the value attached to boys are some of the practices and norms that Adichie challenges in her two novels. She advocates for a world without such oppressive practices.

Adichie's novels are a clarion call to all women to realise that they can live comfortably without being attached to the cultural beliefs and obligations which control women's lives.

Some of the constricting believes which confer titles to males only (like *Omelora* and *ima mmuo*) is deconstructed and instead women made heroines in the two novels. Ifeoma does not attach too much importance to the *ima mmuo* ritual. In doing so she passes a message across that such titles serve to degrade women and they have no place in a progressive society.

References

1. Chaman Nahal, *"Feminisms in English Fiction–Forms & Variants in feminisms and Recent Fiction in English"*, Ed. Sushila Singh, New Delhi, Prestigious book, Pp. 17, 1991.

2. Smacks Patricia, *"Stage of Self: Notes on autobiography and the life cycle in the American autobiographies"*, Pen Craft, Washington DC, Pp.48, 1989

3. Dr. Gunjan Sushila, *"Deshpande Shashi , Roots and Shadows-A feminist Study"*, Ed. Amaranth Prasad, Swroop Book, New Delhi, Pp. 129, 2009.

4. Deshpande Shashi, Interview with M Rati.

5. Ashok Kumar, *"Portrayal of New women-A study of Manju Kapur A married Women"*, Indian ink , New Delhi, Pp.90,1998.

6. Bhagwat Naik, *"Feminine Asserssion in Manju Kapur's, 'A married women' ' The Indian Journal of English studies '*, R.K. Dhawan, Ed New Delhi, IAEI, Pp.13, 2003"

7. Roy Arundhati, *"An Ordinary person's guide to Europe"*, Penguin, New Delhi, 2005.

8. Ibid, Pp.65.

9. Prasad Amaranth, *"Arundhati Roy life, Mind and Art – New lights on Indian Women Novelist In English"*, Part 3, Swroop and Sons New Delhi, Pp. 110, 2005.

10. Arundhati Roy, *"The End of Imagination"*, D C books, Kottpayam, Pp. 53, 1998.

11. Sunaina Singh, *"The novels of Margaret Atwood, And Anita Desai -A comparative study in Feminist Perspective"*, Creative books New Delhi, Pp. 98, 1994.

12. Simon De, Beauvoir, *"The second sex"*, Cambridge, London, Pp.76, 1949.

13. Jasbir Jain, *"Stairs to the Attic: The novel of Anita Desai"*, Jaipur, Princely Publication, Pp. 19, 1987.

14. Anita Desai, Cry, The Peacock (New Delhi: Orient paper backs 1995) Pp.120, 1995.

15. Mukherjee shubha, *"Kautilya's Concept of Diplomacy: A new Interpretation"*, Minerva, 1976.

16. Rushdie Salman, *"The Art of Critical Appreciations of Indian Novelists"* , Starred Reviews, London, 2008.

17. Adichie, Chimamanda Ngozi, "Purple Hibiscus", London: Harper Perennial, 2003.

18. _______________ . Half of a Yellow Sun, Nairobi: Kwani Trust, 2006.

Secondary Texts

1. Abrahams, Howard, *"Glossary of Literary Terms"*, 6th Edition, Fort Worth: Harcourt Brace College Press, 1993.

2. Achebe, Chinua, "Anthills of the Savannah", New York: Doubleday, 1988.

3. _________. The Trouble with Nigeria, Edinburgh Gate: Heinemann, 1983.

4. _________. Things Fall Apart, Oxford: Heinemann, 1958.

5. Acholonu, Catherine, *"Motherism: The Afrocentric Alternative to Feminism"*, Owerri: Afa Publications, 1995.

6. Adetola, Olatunde, *"Man and Society in Africa: An Introduction to Sociology"*, London: Longman, 1983.

7. Aidoo, Ama Ata, *"Literature, Feminism and the African Woman Today"*, Reconstructing Womanhood, Reconstructing Feminism (Ed.) Delia Jarrett-Macauley, London: Routeledge, Pp.156-74, 1996.

8. Amuta, Chidi, *"The Theory of African Literature"*, London and New York: Zed Books, 1989.

9. Anyokwu, Christopher, *"May we Always Remember." Memory and Nationhood in Chimamanda Ngozi Adichie"s Half of a Yellow Sun"*, NTU studies in Language and Literature 20, Pp.179-196, 2008.

10. Arndt, susan, "African Gender Trouble and African Womanism, An Interview With Chikwenye Ogunyemi and Wanjira Muthoni" Signs. Chicago: The University of Chicago Press, 25 (3), Pp.709-726, 2000.

11. Badejo, Dieree, *"African Feminism: Mythical and Social Power of Women of African Descent"*, African Gender Research, 2(1), 22-48, 1999.

12. Ba, Mariama, *"So Long a Letter"*, Ibadan: New Horn Press, 1980. _________.

13. *"Scarlet Song"*, Ibadan: New Horn Press, 1981.

14. Boehmer, Elleke, *"Colonial and Postcolonial literature: Migrant Metaphors"*, Oxford: Oxford University Press, 2005.

15. Chodorow, Nancy, *"The Reproduction of Mothering: Psychoanalysis and Psychology of Gender"*, Berkeley: University of California Press, 1978.

16. Woolf Virginia, *"A Room of One's Own"*, Pen Craft, London, 1929.